Tax Guide 302

LIVING
WILLS &
TRUSTS

by

Holmes F. Crouch
Tax Specialist

Published by

Allyear Tax Guides

20484 Glen Brae Drive
Saratoga, CA 95070

Copyright © 2005 by Holmes F. Crouch
All Rights Reserved

This book may not be reproduced in whole or part, by photocopying or any other means, without the express written permission of the author. Furthermore, this book is sold with the express understanding that the author is not engaged in rendering legal, accounting, or other professional service. The only warranty made is your money back on the cost of purchasing this book.

ISBN 0944817742

LCCN 2005920207

Printed in U.S.A.

Series 300
Retirees & Estates

Tax Guide 302

LIVING WILLS & TRUSTS

LISLE LIBRARY DISTRICT
LISLE, ILLINOIS 60532

For other titles in print, see page 224.

346.052
con

The author: **Holmes F. Crouch**
For more about the author, see page 221.

PREFACE

If you are a knowledge-seeking **taxpayer** looking for information, this book can be helpful to you. It is designed to be read — from cover to cover — in about eight hours. Or, it can be "skim-read" in about 30 minutes.

Either way, you are treated to **tax knowledge** . . . *beyond the ordinary*. The "beyond" is that which cannot be found in IRS publications, the IRS web site, IRS e-file instructions, or tax software programs.

Taxpayers have different levels of interest in a selected subject. For this reason, this book starts with introductory fundamentals and progresses onward. You can verify the progression by chapter and section in the table of contents. In the text, "applicable law" is quoted in pertinent part. Key phrases and key tax forms are emphasized. Real-life examples are given . . . in down-to-earth style.

This book has 12 chapters. This number provides depth without cross-subject rambling. Each chapter starts with a head summary of meaningful information.

To aid in your skim-reading, informative diagrams and tables are placed strategically throughout the text. By leafing through page by page, reading the summaries and section headings, and glancing at the diagrams and tables, you can get a good handle on the matters covered.

Effort has been made to update and incorporate all of the latest tax law changes that are *significant* to the title subject. However, "beyond the ordinary" does not encompass every conceivable variant of fact and law that might give rise to protracted dispute and litigation. Consequently, if a particular statement or paragraph is crucial to your own specific case, you are urged to seek professional counseling. Otherwise, the information presented is general and is designed for a broad range of reader interests.

The Author

INTRODUCTION

The term "living," as we use it, pertains to the preparation of a testamentary instrument — either a will or a trust — while the maker/creator thereof is alive. The term has no cutesy meaning other than this one basic fact: That you are alive . . . with sound mind . . . and knowing it. There are other meanings to the terms "living wills" and "living trusts," which we'll describe when appropriate. Otherwise, our focus in this book is strictly on the distinguishing features between wills and trusts that you need to know when preparing them.

While you are living, your prepared instrument can be changed at any time, for any reason. This is the *revocability feature* of a living instrument. Revocability assumes that you know what you are doing and that senile dementia has not set in to deprive you of testamentary capacity. *Testamentary capacity* requires particularly that you comprehend the nature (real, tangible, intangible) and extent (degree of ownership) of your property holdings. It also requires that you be cognizant of the persons or entities to whom you gratuitously convey your property upon your demise. At time of death, your living instruments become irrevocable.

When giving property to others after your death, there is an *accountability* requirement to be met. That is, you can give only that which you own, and then only after an inventory and appraisement has been made and after all debts, expenses, and taxes have been reconciled. The effect is that your estate is put on "hold" until all accountability issues have been settled. This takes time — between 9 and 15 months ordinarily — regardless of who prepares a will or a trust, you or an attorney.

Whether you or an attorney prepares a testamentary instrument, much depends on the value of your distributable estate and on the degree of responsibleness of your intended recipients. If you have a small estate (less than $1,000,000), a will could serve you well. If you have a modest estate (up to $3,000,000), some combination of a will and joint tenancy, or of a will and a short-term trust, can avoid probate and expedite your bequests to mature adults. For estates above $3,000,000, an ongoing trust is more wise.

Whereas a will is the one-time conveyance of your "distributable assets," a trust is conveyance of the same assets over an extended period of time: 5 , 10 , 25 years, . . . or longer. Whereas a will can run three to five pages in length (including witnessing), a trust might run 35 to 50 pages in length. Because of distributive projections over time, a trust requires far more contingency clauses than does a will. For example, suppose you have a minor-age daughter to whom you have directed certain property interests. Distribution wise, what happens when said daughter becomes an adult, marries, bears children, gets divorced, gets remarried, and bears a second crop of children? A trust enables you to more readily provide for these contingencies than does a will.

With either instrument, there is — or can be — probative issues. Probate, as you may already know, is the process of proving the validity of a will or that of a trust **after** the demise of the will maker (testator) or of the trust creator (trustor). Probate can be, though it need not always be, a protracted and litigious gaming for the spoils of your estate. The process can dramatically reduce the amount available for distribution to your designatees. A living trust can do more towards eliminating (or at least minimizing) the probative aspects than can a will.

And then, also, there is the taxation process. Contrary to the impression often fueled by professional trust preparers, trusts cannot eliminate nor reduce taxation matters that must be addressed after death. There are personal income tax returns for you as the decedent that have to be finalized. There are income tax returns for your estate and, separately, income tax returns for your trust, that have to be prepared. If your estate exceeds $1,500,000 (in 2004 and 2005), or $2,000,000 (in 2006, 2007 and 2008), there is a death (transfer) tax return to be prepared. The death tax rates are significantly higher than income tax rates. There is no escaping it. Death and taxes will never go away.

In short, there is much you need to know about testamentary documentation. Attorneys and estate professionals do not always explain adequately the various ramifications to you. It is this void — and this void only — that we try to fill with this book.

CONTENTS

Chapter   **Page**

1. INTESTATE SUCCESSION **1-1**

    Absence of a Will is Key 1- 2
    Probate Procedures Apply 1- 4
    Surviving Spouse Protection 1- 5
    Separate Property of Decedent Spouse 1- 8
    When No Surviving Spouse 1- 9
    More on Predeceased Spouse   1-11
    Escheat of Decedent's Property   1-13

2. TESTATORS & TRUSTORS **2-1**

    Freedom of Testation 2- 2
    Testamentary Capacity 2- 3
    Tests for Soundness 2- 4
    Example Preamble by Testator 2- 6
    Make Revocations as Backup 2- 7
    Trust Titling Options 2- 9
    Example Preamble by Trustor(s)   2-12
    Signaturizing & Witnessing   2-13

3. FEATURES OF A WILL **3-1**

    Purpose & Contents 3- 2
    Construction & Interpretation 3- 3
    Joint Wills: No-No 3- 6
    Simultaneous Deaths 3- 7
    Percentages or Dollars? 3- 9
    The Disinheritance Clause   3-12
    Holographic Wills   3-13
    Statutory Will Forms   3-14
    Attorney Not Necessary   3-15
    Nonprobate Transfers   3-18

Chapter		Page

4. FEATURES OF A TRUST **4-1**

State Law Provisions 4- 2
Manifestation of Intent.. 4- 4
Designation of Trust Property 4- 6
A "Pots and Pans" Will.. 4- 7
Avoidance of Probate 4- 8
While Both Trustees Alive 4-12
Subtrusts for First Decedent...................................... 4-13
Death of Surviving Trustor... 4-15
Successor Trustees & Powers..................................... 4-16
Designation of Beneficiaries....................................... 4-18
Should Limit the Number.. 4-19
Contingency Clauses Ad Nauseum.......................... 4-21
Rule Against Perpetuities.. 4-23

5. WILLS & TRUSTS COMPARED........... **5-1**

Identical Soundness of Mind....................................... 5- 2
Estate Accounting the Same....................................... 5- 3
Distribution Time Difference....................................... 5- 5
Dollar Value Distinctions?... 5- 7
Wills are Simply Simpler... 5- 9
Estates Under $100,000 5-11
Best Argument for a Trust.. 5-12
Certification of Trust.. 5-14
Organizational Formalities... 5-15

6. EXECUTOR, TRUSTEE ROLES............ **6-1**

Appointment Process: Executor.............................. 6- 2
Appointment Process: Trustee................................. 6- 3
Duties & Powers of Executor 6- 5
Role of "Letters Testamentary"................................... 6- 6
IRS Form 706: Yes or No?.. 6- 9
Income Transition Form 1041.................................... 6-10
Identification Duty of Trustee...................................... 6-12
Trustee as "Investment Manager"............................... 6-13
Annual Use of Form 1041 6-15

Chapter		Page

7. OTHER LIVING OPTIONS............... **7-1**

Joint Tenancy: WROS...	7- 2
Probate Avoidance Only...	7- 4
Some Practical Examples...	7- 5
Retained Life Estate...	7- 6
Annual Exclusion Gifts..	7- 8
Larger Gifts Permitted...	7-10
Tracking Taxable Gifts..	7-11
Grant of Certain Powers..	7-14

8. KNOWING YOUR PROPERTY............ **8-1**

Realty and Personalty...	8- 2
Four Classes Defined...	8- 3
Separate Ownership of Property.............................	8- 5
Husband and Wife Property.....................................	8- 7
Joint Tenancy vs. Tenancy in Common....................	8- 9
IRS Property Schedules..	8-11
Schedules B & C: Intangibles.................................	8-13
Schedule D — Life Insurance..................................	8-14
Schedules E & F — Other Property Items...............	8-15
Schedules G, H, & I..	8-16

9. IDENTIFYING DISTRIBUTEES........... **9-1**

Cite Family Status First..	9- 2
Clarifying Other Names..	9- 4
Deceased Married Child..	9- 5
Divorce and Remarriage...	9- 7
5 Classes of Children..	9- 9
Married Without Children.......................................	9-11
Unmarried: No Children, No Siblings.....................	9-13
Precautions with Charities......................................	9-14
Abuse of Charity Example......................................	9-16
Generation-Skipping Transfers................................	9-17

Chapter		Page
10.	**THE PROBATE PROCESS**	**10-1**
	The Purpose of Probate	10- 2
	Pre-Visit the Probate Court	10- 3
	Check-the-Box Type Forms	10- 6
	Starting the Process	10- 8
	Taking Possession of Estate	10-11
	Meaning of "Independent Administration"	10-12
	Final Accounting & Disposition	10-15
11.	**THE TAXATION PROCESS**	**11-1**
	Start with Form SS-4	11- 3
	Information Returns: Forms 1099	11- 4
	Form 1040 vs. Form 1041	11- 6
	Death Year 1040 "Final"	11- 8
	Short Span of Estate 1041	11- 9
	Role of Schedule K-1	11-10
	Transfer Taxation: 3 Kinds	11-10
	Form 706: "Yes" or "No"	11-12
	When No Form 706 Required	11-15
12.	**WRITING YOUR OWN WILL**	**12-1**
	Sample Preamble Wording	12- 2
	Revocation is "First"	12- 3
	Declaration of Heirs: "Second"	12- 5
	Appointment of Executor: "Third"	12- 6
	Delegation of Powers: "Fourth"	12- 7
	Declaration of Property: "Fifth"	12- 9
	Declaration of Gifts, etc.: "Sixth"	12-10
	Bequests to Spouse: "Seventh"	12-12
	Common Disaster Clause: "Eighth"	12-13
	Young Adults & Spendthrifts: "Ninth"	12-15
	Minors & Disabled: "Tenth"	12-17
	Bequests to Others: "Eleventh"	12-19
	The $1 Clause: "Twelfth"	12-21
	The Witness Paragraph	12-22

1

INTESTATE SUCCESSION

If You Die Without A Will, Laws Of Intestate Succession Mandate To Whom Your Property Shall Be Distributed. As To Community Property, Your Surviving Spouse Gets All. As To Separate Property, Your Surviving Spouse Shares With Your Surviving Children Or Grandchildren. If No Surviving Spouse Or Children, Lines Of Kinship Must Be Traced, Starting With Parents On Down, Then Grandparents On Down, Then Great Grandparents On Down. If No Legal Heir Or Kin Can Be Found, All Of Your Property (After Claims, Taxes, & Expenses) Escheats (Reverts) To That State Government From Which Your Property Rights Arose.

The general idea behind having a will and/or a trust is to direct the distribution of your property after your demise. With either of these two instruments, you can designate to whom the property is to be distributed, and how much to each. You can do this whether your designees are your legal heirs or not As used in the context here, the word "property" is that which has marketable value to persons other than those whom you choose as its recipients. This eliminates dispositional concern for personal clothing, household linens, homemade artifacts, and family memorabilia (photos, letters, etc.). It is *property of value* in which both recipients and tax authorities have a financial interest after you die.

But, suppose you have no will or trust. What happens then? Or, what happens if your will or trust is invalid? Or, what happens if either is valid, but significant portions of your property holdings are not expressly earmarked therein?

Answer: The law of intestate succession kicks in. The term "intestate" is the condition of having died without leaving a will.

In such case, the laws of succession, laws of inheritance, and laws of descent and distribution (of property) prevail. These laws differ in different states throughout the U.S., and in different countries of the world. Much depends on the domicile (principal residence) of the decedent, and on the physical location of real property such as land, structures thereon, and natural resources thereof. All such laws have three purposes in common. They are: (1) To establish the legitimacy of an heir or heirs; (2) to assure that all relevant financial, accounting, and tax matters have been addressed before the property passes to intestate sharers; and (3) if no intestate sharers, to establish procedures for conveying property to that state from which the original property rights arose.

Accordingly, in this our introductory chapter, we want to touch on the highlights of intestate succession, on its underlying principles, and on what happens if no intestate sharer can be located. No one with property of value intentionally wants to be intestate. Nevertheless, sometimes death happens before one is estate-prepared for it. If nothing else, the material we present in this chapter is foundationally instructive. It will help you to understand better the importance of our subsequent chapters.

> *Editorial Note*: In order to properly illustrate certain points in this and other chapters, it is necessary to cite related legal rules. As our source for these citations, we have chosen the Probate Code for the State of California. Other state probate rules may — and most likely do — differ.

Absence of a Will is Key

While a trust can be useful as an estate-planning tool, it is not a prerequisite for establishing whether or not the rules of intestacy apply. A will is, but not a trust. As clear evidence of this, we cite from two selected sections of the California Probate Code [CPC]. Our first citation is Section 6400: *Property subject to intestacy provisions*. Its full 24 words read—

Any part of the estate of a decedent not effectively disposed of by will passes to the decedent's heirs as prescribed in this part [Wills and Intestate Succession].

While CPC Section 6400 does not expressly say "in the absence of," CPC Section 7000 definitely does. Section 7000: *Passage to devisee or intestate heirs*, reads for the most part as—

*Title to a decedent's property passes on the decedent's death to the person to whom it is devised in the decedent's last will or, **in the absence of** such a devise, to the decedent's heirs as prescribed in the laws governing intestate succession.* [Emphasis added.]

In either of these two citations, is there any reference to a trust? Obviously not. This means that of the two testamentary-type instruments, one's will — or absence of it — dominates the property-distribution concerns moments after one's death. Why do you think this is so?

Answer: When a person dies, his/her estate — all of it — is "frozen in place," so to speak. No distributee can claim his or her share of said property until the following events are closed:

1. There is a complete inventory and appraisement (valuation) of said property: real, tangible, intangible, and personal.

2. All debts owed **by** the decedent are ascertained and paid, or other satisfactory methods are made to do so.

3. All attempts have been made to claim and collect any money and/or property due the decedent.

4. All potential heirs of at least one generation above and one generation below that of the decedent are located and identified.

5. All federal and state taxation matters — income, inheritance, and employer-related — are duly reported and finalized.

All of the above events take place under the operation of state law where the decedent resided and where his or her real property (if any) is located. The procedures for doing so take more than a few weeks and often more than several months of time. Meanwhile, the distribution-of-property process is suspended.

Probate Procedures Apply

Over the years, the word "probate" has acquired an ugly and sinister meaning. It raises concerns about legal cronyism, avaricious attorneys, and grave robbing by distant relatives. Over the same years, fortunately, judicial wisdom has evolved. There are now common-sense procedures for distributing property of value after an intestator dies. By the way, "to probate" means to prove that some property item is genuine, that some legitimate heir exists, and that some material fact (such as, money owing **to** the decedent or money owed **by** the decedent) can be realistically confirmed.

Establishing the necessary proving, often — but not always — requires judicial proceedings in the Probate Court having jurisdiction where the decedent was domiciled. The cost of all forms of this proving: fiduciary fees, attorney fees, accounting fees, tax preparer fees, probate referee fees, and directly related expenses, are, after taxes, a priority deduction against the intestator's estate. Creditors are the next priority, contracts (including other written obligations of the decedent) are next. After all estate affairs are settled, each heir (legatee, distributee) then receives his or her proportionate share of the residual estate.

Formal proceedings in Probate Court are not always necessary. Especially so, if the decedent's state of domicile has some form of *small estate* rule. In California, for example, there is such a set of rules collectively titled: *Disposition of Estate without Administration* [CPC Sections 13000 through 13660]. Its Part 1 is titled: *Collection or Transfer of Small Estate without Administration*. Its Part 2 is titled: *Passage of Property to Surviving Spouse without Administration*. You've probably already gathered that the term "without administration" means without instituting probative procedures and (perhaps) even without an attorney.

The essence of a small estate boils down to this—

1. Registered vehicles, vessels, and mobile homes (campers, houseboats, manufactured homes, trailers) may pass to the holders of said property subject to the right-of-proof by each applicable state licensing agency.

2. The collection or transfer of personal property (other than item 1) not exceeding $100,000 in value, may pass via an Affidavit Procedure (declaration) by the holder(s) of the decedent's property other than real estate.

3. An affidavit procedure for real property not exceeding $20,000 in value.

4. Husband or wife dying intestate; surviving spouse; administration not necessary where property (especially real property) is titled as community property or as quasi-community property.

For other than the above small estate cases, a formal petition for probate is necessary. This requires the engagement of an attorney, and is beyond our discussion here.

As a depictional summary of where we are at this point, we present Figure 1.1. The idea being presented is that, if you are the *personal representative* for the decedent, you have a responsibility to fulfill before any of the decedent's estate can be distributed.

Surviving Spouse Protection

The underlying principle of intestate succession laws is family continuity and protection. Intestacy death was never intended to deprive the surviving spouse, minor children, and disabled dependents of any and all rights to the decedent's property. If a decedent was married at time of death, intestacy provisions protect foremost the surviving spouse. In California, for example, intestate sharing is predicated upon the doctrine of community property and quasi-community property.

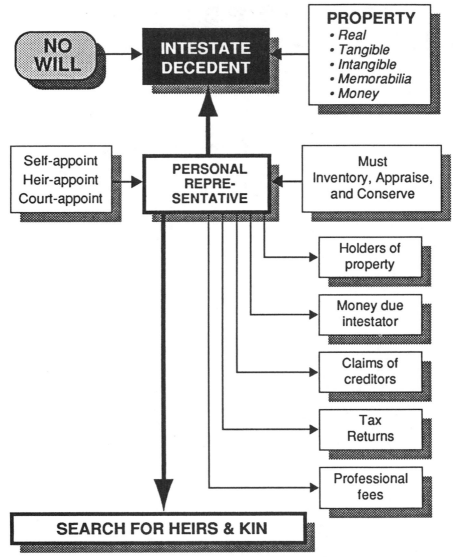

Fig. 1.1 - The "Suspension Aspects" of Intestator's Property

Community property is based on the concept that all property acquired during marriage is due to the joint effort of both spouses. It doesn't matter which spouse actually earned the money for acquiring the property. Nor does it matter that the property carries both spouses' names or not. It belongs one-half to each. Currently, eight states have adopted the community property doctrine. Other states have adopted *equitable distribution* statutes which accomplish much the same result as community property. Quasi-community property is a variant concept where property is acquired in a non-community property state (while married) and the intestator dies while both are domiciled in a community property state.

With this background in mind, two specific California Probate Code rules apply. They are CPC Sections 6401(a) and 6401(b). Each reads succinctly—

(a) *As to **community property**, the intestate share of the surviving spouse is the one-half of the community property that belongs to the decedent.*

(b) *As to **quasi-community property**, the intestate share of the surviving spouse is the one-half of the quasi-community property that belongs to the decedent.*

The only succession condition is that the intestator be legally married as husband or wife at time of death. The spouses may have been physically separated, or they may have been in the throes of divorce. The fact that the marriage has not been legally terminated is controlling. The fact that the spouses may not have filed a joint income tax return (federal or state) is not controlling. Each could have filed "married filing separately" or not have filed at all. It's the legal status of marriage at time of death that counts. California has a domestic partners law which extends to such partners the same intestate succession rights of a married couple. Indeed CPC Section 6401 is expressly titled: *Surviving spouse **or surviving domestic partner**; intestate share*; etc.

In other words, if there is any form of co-ownership of property between spouses or domestic partners (in California), whether actual or implied, the survivor gets it all. Furthermore if the intestator transferred property to a person (a transferee) other than to the survivor, without receiving valuable consideration for it, CPC Section 102 applies. This is called the "restoration rule." Under this rule, the survivor may require the transferee to restore to the decedent's estate one-half of said property or one-half of its value at the time of transfer. Thus, a surviving spouse or domestic partner is truly a protected party under California intestate succession law.

Separate Property of Decedent Spouse

Even in California, separate property of a married person who is deceased may exist. Property acquired by the decedent *before* marriage is his or her own separate property. That which is acquired by *gift* from other than the spouse, while married, is separate property. That which is acquired by *bequest* upon the death of some other person is also separate property.

There are identity problems with separate property in a community property state. One problem is the high likelihood of *commingling* both kinds of property while married. This is a matter of pure convenience, without giving any thought to the possibility of death (or of divorce). Another problem is the high likelihood of *not having good records* on the acquisition dates and amounts of alleged separate property. Nevertheless, if the existence of separate property of the deceased spouse can be reasonably established, CPC § 6401(c) comes into play.

> *Editorial Note*: From this point on, we'll use the symbol § to substitute for the word: "section." California uses this symbol consistently through its probate code.

As cited in full, CPC § 6401(c) reads—

(c) As to separate property [of the intestator], *the intestate share of the surviving spouse is—*

> *(1) The entire intestate estate if the decedent did not leave any surviving issue* [children], *parent, brother, sister, or issue of a deceased brother or sister.*

> *(2) One-half of the intestate estate—*

> *(A) Where the decedent leaves only one child or the issue of one deceased child.*

(B) Where the decedent leaves no issue but leaves a parent or parents or their issue or the issue of either of them.

(3) One-third of the intestate estate—

(A) Where the decedent leaves more than one child.
(B) Where the decedent leaves one child and the issue of one or more deceased children.
(C) Where the decedent leaves issue of two or more deceased children.

From a careful re-reading of the above, you can get the general sense of what intestate succession is all about. It is predicated upon the "next of kin" tracing down a generational line. First are children of the decedent, then issue of a deceased child. If a child is still alive, that child's children do not participate in intestate succession. The idea is to exhaust one generational line before going on to another generational line.

Let us illustrate the case of CPC § 6401(c)(3) cited above. Suppose the deceased spouse has three children, one of whom is deceased. That deceased child has two children living. The intestate sharing percentages of the decedent's separate property are portrayed in Figure 1.2. As you can see, the surviving spouse gets one-third, or 33.33%. Everyone else gets a total of two thirds, or 66.66%. The two surviving children each get 22.22%; the two issue of the deceased child each get 11.11%. When we add up all five heirs, what do we get?

Answer: 33.33% + 22.22% + 22.22% + 11.11% + 11.11% = 99.99%, or 100% when rounded.

These percentages hold regardless of age, health, or financial need of the recipients. Without any testamentary guidance to the contrary, this is the mandate of state law.

When No Surviving Spouse

The citations above are predicated upon there being a surviving spouse. What happens if the decedent's spouse predeceased him or her? What happens if the decedent and spouse were divorced before the decedent's death? Or, what happens if the decedent intestator never married?

Answer: In California, CPC § 6402 takes front and center. This section is titled: *Intestate estate not passing to surviving spouse*. It comprises approximately 500 words. The succession rules start getting more complicated.

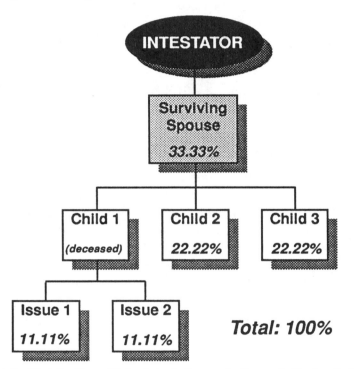

Fig. 1.2 - Distribution of Intestator's Separate Property Under California Law

To give you the flavor of the complexity involved, we cite selected portions of the first few paragraphs of CPC § 6402:

If there is no surviving spouse, the entire intestate estate passes—

(a) To the issue of the decedent, the issue taking equally if they are all of the same degree of kinship to the decedent . . .

*(b)   If there is **no surviving issue**, to the decedent's parent or parents equally.*

*(c)   If there is **no surviving issue or parent**, to the issue of the parents or either of them, the issue taking equally if they are all of the same degree of kinship to the decedent . . .*

(d)   . . . grandparents . . . or issue thereof . . .
(e)   . . . issue of a predeceased spouse . . .
(f)   . . . nearest ancestral kin of decedent . . .
(g)   . . . nearest ancestral kin of predeceased spouse . . .
. . . and so on.

The effort that goes into locating an eligible nest of kin can get quite out of hand. It focuses on each *degree of kinship* to the decedent, then going down that generational line until at least one living kin can be located and confirmed. There are three degrees of kinship: parents, grandparents, and great grandparents. As we depict in Figure 1.3, tracking down each of three generational lines can be a daunting challenge. To really appreciate what we mean, we urge that you take a moment to actually read down the list of kinships depicted. The idea is to locate at least one living kin, then search for others of the same level. And then share equally.

Our Figure 1.3 presumes that there is no predeceased spouse of the intestate decedent. If there were such a spouse, the great-grandparent kinship line would be abandoned. In its place, the kinship lines of the parents and grandparents of the predeceased spouse would be pursued.

More on Predeceased Spouse

California intestate succession law defines a predeceased person as one who does not survive the decedent by 120 hours [CPC § 6403]. This is the equivalent of five days (that is, five full 24-hour days). The legal counting measure is *hours*: not days. When one dies, his/her date and hour of death are recorded on the death certificate. Suppose, for example, that an intestator died at 11:20 a.m. on Day 1. If his spouse died at 11:30 a.m. on Day 5 (10

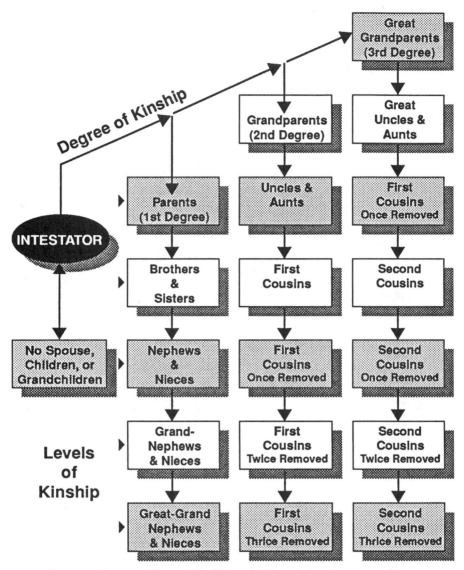

Fig. 1.3 - Tracing Next of Kin When No Surviving Spouse or Issue

minutes more than 120 hours), she would be the surviving spouse. But if she died at 11:10 a.m. on Day 5 (10 minutes *less* than 120 hours), she would be a predeceased spouse. Different intestate succession rules apply.

A predeceased spouse, for division of property purposes, is accorded the benefits of CPC § 6402.5. This probate code section is titled: *Predeceased spouse: portion of decedent's estate attributable to decedent's predeceased spouse.* The idea — throughout the about 1,400 statutory words — is to permit certain heirs of the predeceased spouse to make claims against the intestate estate of the decedent.

Subsection (**a**) of § 6402.5 focuses on real property whereas subsection (**b**) focuses on personal property (all that which is not real property).

CPC § 6402.5(**a**) reads in part as—

*For purposes of distributing **real property** . . . if the decedent had a predeceased spouse who died **not more than fifteen years before the decedent, and there is no surviving spouse or issue** of the decedent, the portion of the decedent's estate attributable to the decedent's predeceased spouse passes as follows:* (1), (2), (3), (4), and (5)

CPC § 6402.5(**b**) reads similarly to that above except that the word "real" is replaced by "personal," and the "15" years is reduced to "5" years. The phrase "portion of the decedent's estate attributable to the decedent's predeceased spouse" means one-half of the community property in existence at the time of death of the predeceased spouse.

In both (a) and (b) cases, the subparagraph (5) directs that if no next of kin of the predeceased spouse can be found, the intestate decedent's property shall escheat to the state of domicile of the predeceased spouse.

Escheat of Decedent's Property

The term "escheat" means the reversion of property to government, when no living heir or kin can be found. The premise of this doctrine is that all human rights to property derive from the laws of government. Therefore, if no legal distributee exists, the property reverts to government after a reasonable period of search time. How much search time is reasonable?

California intestate succession law does not expressly state how long is a reasonable search time. For small intestate estates (less than $100,000), customary practice suggests that two years after the intestator's death is reasonable. For larger estates, three years appears to be quite adequate.

To which government does the property escheat? There can be as many as three different governmental jurisdictions. Foremost would be the state of domicile where the intestator died. Next would be the state of jurisdiction over the decedent's real property, should it be noncurrent with his state of death. A third possibility is the state where the decedent's tangible personal property (vehicles, motor homes, trailers) is customarly registered. Intangible personal property (bank accounts, mutual funds, stock portfolios) belong to the state where the decedent last domiciled.

The essence of California escheat law lies in CPC § 6800: *Failure to leave person to take by intestate succession; escheat.* Its introductory wording reads in part—

> *If a decedent, whether or not* [he/she] *was domiciled in* [California], *leaves no one to take the decedent's estate or any portion thereof, . . . by intestate succession, the property escheats . . . to this state.*

CPC § 6806 provides an interesting twist to the general escheat rule above. This section is titled: *Property distributable from trusts; benefit plans; reversion to trust or fund from which distributable*. The essence of its first sentence reads—

> *Notwithstanding any other provison of* [California] *law, a benefit consisting of money or other property distributable from a trust established under a plan providing health and welfare, pension, vacation, retirement, or similar benefits **does not pass to or escheat to** this state . . . but goes to the trust or fund from which it is distributable.*

This is the only place in California's intestate succession law where the word "trust" is mentioned. All other references to testamentary-type instruments refer to one's will.

2

TESTATORS & TRUSTORS

Every Owner Of Property Is Free To Distribute It
Gratuitously, After His Death, To A Person Or Persons Of
His Choice. If He Does So Via A WILL, He Is The Testator
(Or Maker) Thereof. If He Does So Via A TRUST, He Is
The Trustor (Or Creator) Thereof. Either Way, He Must
Be Of SOUND MIND And Understand What He Intends To
Do: Either Give It Away All At Once, Or Convey It By
Contract Over Time. He Can Proclaim His State Of Mind
With Preamble Wording, And Reaffirm It When
Completing His Testamentary Documents. For A Will,
He Needs Two Ordinary Witnesses; For A Trust,
Attestation By A Notary Public Is More Effective.

A "testator" is the *maker of a will*; a "trustor" is the *creator of a trust*. One "makes" a will because after the testator's death, his/her will directs distribution of property more or less at one time. One "creates" a trust because after the trustor's death, his/her trust directs distribution of property — and the income from it — over an extended period of time. In other words, a testator makes a one-time testament whereas a trustor makes an ongoing testament. A trustor has to create a legal entity for doing so.

Stated another way, a testator thinks in terms of *short-term* distributions of property. A trustor thinks in terms of *long-term distributions*. This is **the** fundamental distinction between testators and trustors, and between wills and trusts. Furthermore, there is no requirement that a testator also prepare a trust. Once all of a testator's property is distributed by will, any need for a trust is moot.

The only exception is where the will directs some portion of the testator's property into his trust. In short, a will precedes a trust; a trust does not precede a will.

In this chapter, therefore, we want to develop the reality that testators and trustors are persons of different mindsets. This is so, even though each may be one and the same in human form and in ownership of property. Our premise is that there are two different "thinking worlds" out there. There are reasons for this, which we feel compelled to tell you about. Too often, professionals (attorneys and estate planners) tend to push at you a raft of testamentary documents which they label as your "estate plan" without adequately explaining what each is about. You are asked to sign this line, that line, and various other lines without really knowing what you are signing and why. We simply want to clarify your different testamentary powers, if we can.

Freedom of Testation

The power of an owner of property to determine who is to have it upon his death is an inalienable right. It derives from the general idea that property consists of a bundle of rights. Among these are the right of possession, use, enjoyment, sale, exchange, gift, rent, loan, divide, and so on. As we have seen in the previous chapter, if one does not provide for the disposition of property in a testamentary document of his own making, the laws of intestate succession prevail. It is a situation where you either use your testamentary power . . . or lose it. Then some state government takes over your property.

One's freedom of testation is not unlimited. For example, you cannot disinherit a surviving spouse. Nor can you disinherit minor children or disabled dependents (regardless of age). You can, however, disinherit adult children and other close kin. If you do, you must do so knowingly with clear declaratory intent. You may demonstrate this clarity by citing some specific reason, without giving all the details. Otherwise, you can designate whomever you want to receive specific items or portions of your property.

You cannot require a testamentary recipient to perform any services for you while alive, or to perform services for others after your demise. Otherwise, you are disguising compensation for services (which is taxable) as a gratuitous gift (which is not taxable). Nor can you impose a condition on the acceptance or use of your property that is unlawful. You can express a preference on how your property should be used, so long as it is clearly an expression of preference only. In all other respects, testamentary transfers of property are classed as *gratuitous transfers*. The term "gratuitous" means that you have conveyed the property post-mortem without any strings attached. By your so doing, the recipient can do whatever he or she wants with your property.

Testamentary power is an *individual* thing. If you are married, you are entitled to distribute your own share of the marital property (plus your separate property) as you see fit. Similarly for your spouse. Each of you has a separate and distinct testamentary capacity. You have one head and one mind, and one set of testamentary preferences. Your spouse also has one head and one mind, etc. You may coordinate your intentions, but they are never joined as one, like that of filing a joint income tax return.

Testamentary Capacity

A testator must have "testamentary capacity." This is defined as being of *sound mind* at the time of drafting a will, trust, or other instrument of gratuitous intent. A sound mind is required because a will or trust is an expression of purpose which has not yet gone into effect. Conveyance of property is only contemplated.

The term "sound mind" means the capacity to comprehend the ordinary affairs of life. This specifically includes knowing the nature and extent of one's property, and knowing those persons who are, or should be, the natural objects of one's affection. Testamentary capacity also includes the comprehension that a will or trust expresses *donative intent at death*. That is, a testator or trustor must be aware that he is passing his assets along to others.

A testator or trustor should know and understand what the contents of his will or trust are, and he must have this understanding at the time such document is prepared. At such time, he must not be mentally incompetent and he must not be acting under the "undue influence" of anyone.

The mere fact that the testator or trustor is under some delusion or misgiving does not affect the validity of his will or trust. To invalidate either, it must be proven that the delusions or misgivings actually constituted the motive for the dispositions made by him. Coaxing and persuasion are generally not held to constitute undue influence unless accompanied by actual threats.

It is true that there are degrees of mental unsoundness and temporary situations which can destroy testamentary capacity. But there is no particular degree of mental ability to serve as a reference standard of competency and soundness. Such a standard is lacking for the simple reason that testamentary capacity is not the same as the ability to transact business agreements, contracts, decisions, and finances. It is only necessary that the testator be aware that he is formulating the property distributions freely in his own mind.

Tests for Soundness

The most common basis for attacking the validity of a will or trust is allegation of deficits in mental functions. A person known to have a mental or physical disorder may still be capable of making testamentary decisions. To establish otherwise, a judicial determination is required. Evidence must be presented that the targeted person is totally without understanding, or is of unsound mind, or suffers from one or more mental deficits so substantial that, under the circumstances, the person should be deemed to lack the requisite legal capacity.

The type of evidence needed to support a judicial finding of unsound mind is prescribed, for example, in California Probate Code Section 811. This section is titled: *Deficits in mental functions*. It consists of approximately 700 words, with subsections on alertness and attention, ability to reason logically, etc. The concluding gist in CPC § 811(d) is that—

The mere diagnosis of a mental or physical disorder shall not be sufficient in and of itself to support a determination that a person is of unsound mind or lacks the capacity to do a certain act [such as to understand the nature and effect of his testament]. [CPC § 811(d).]

The type of evidence needed to support a judicial finding of unsound mind is digested from CPC § 811 and tabulated in Figure 2.1. No one "testing factor" is determinative by itself. Two or more of such factors must conjoin to indicate substantial impairment of one's overall mental capabilities.

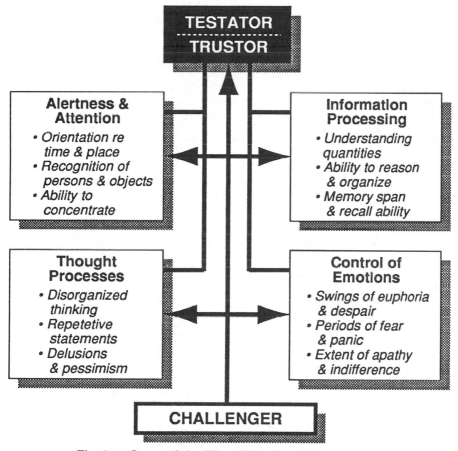

Fig. 2.1 - Some of the "Tests" for Soundness of Mind

To prove any allegation of unsound mental state, the person or entity with a legitimate financial interest in the decedent's property must come forward with evidence. To do this properly, a formal petition in the Probate Court having jurisdiction over the decedent's property must be filed. After giving due public notice of the probate hearing, each side then explains its first-hand observations.

Example Preamble by Testator

There is one very positive feature of a will or trust. The testator or trustor can throw down the gauntlet at any would-be challenger. This is done in the preamble wording of each such testamentary instrument. The wording differs for each instrument. We illustrate the testator's case first.

A will is not enforceable or challengeable until after its maker's death. For this reason, every will must be identified by the personal name of its maker. For illustration purposes only, let us assume that the testator's name is John Quincy Jones. This name is purely a fictitious selection on our part. Accordingly, John's will would be titled as—

LAST WILL AND TESTAMENT

OF

JOHN QUINCY JONES

With this title wording, there should be no question about whose will is being challenged. If John had a wife at the time, her will would be titled separately. Suppose her name was Mary Jane Jones. Then, her will would be titled—

LAST WILL AND TESTAMENT

OF

MARY JANE JONES

By this separate titling, John could be found to be mentally impaired, for example, without affecting Mary's testamentary intentions. Though perhaps coordinated, the two wills are not conjoined in any single challengeable way.

Immediately following John's title of his will, he proclaims—

I, JOHN QUINCY JONES, a resident of Redding, County of Shasta, State of California, being of sound and disposing mind and memory, and not acting under duress, menace, fraud, or undue influence of any person whomsoever, do make, publish, and declare this to be my Last Will and Testament, in the manner and form following, to wit:

If John had an alias and maintained legal residence in two different states, the leadoff sentence in his preamble might read as—

I, JOHN QUINCY JONES, also known as JACK GREEN BROWN, a resident of Redding, County of Shasta, State of California, also a resident of Glendale, County of Maricopa, State of Arizona, being of sound and disposing mind and memory . . .

You get the idea, do you not? John is saying: "Hey, I know what I am doing, and I am doing it voluntarily."

Make Revocations as Backup

There is one favorite "hat trick" used by attorneys when challenging a will. It is to dig through old papers and documents of a testamentary nature that the testator may have signed many years — 5, 10, 15, or so — before his current will. It could be an old will; it could be an insurance policy; it could be a joint account of some sort; or it could be a handwritten note promising some property item to a close kin not named in the current will. Such items often are introduced as evidence of mental unsoundness by the testator. To counter this type of evidential possibility, one or more *revocation clauses* are used.

There is true wisdom in a revocation clause. It enables the testator to clear away all prior "promises," whether written or oral, and whether forgotten, misplaced, or destroyed. A revocation clause may be general, or it may be specific, or both. If a specific revocation is intended, it should follow the general revocation. The "specifics" refer to an actual prior testamentary document, its date, and its place of execution.

To illustrate our point, let us continue with John Quincy Jones. The very first paragraph of his will should emphatically read—

FIRST

I hereby revoke any and all former Wills, codicils to Wills, and Testamentary Dispositions by me at any time heretofore made. (General)

and (as applicable)

I specifically revoke my former Will dated April 22, 2003 executed at Denver, Colorado. (Specific)

A "codicil" is an amendment, supplement, or change to an existing will, usually limited to one or two clarifications only. A "testamentary disposition" refers to holographic wills, oral promises, and other instances of prior testamentary intentions.

In some cases, a former will may contain a testamentary trust (created at time of death) so that it stands apart from the will itself. Typical situations include a special needs trust (for a disabled person) an educational trust, and/or a spendthrift trust. If the trusts are revocable, or if they take effect only upon death, a testator may wish to revoke one or more of said trusts. In this case, he may add to the above—

and (as applicable)

I specifically revoke that Testamentary Trust (with spendthrift provisions for my son) described by that instrument dated March 14, 2004 executed at Houston, Texas.

Also, a testator may have formulated an inter vivos trust (between living persons) as a will substitute and as a means of avoiding the complications of probate at death. A living trust is revocable at any time during the life of the trustor. Therefore, if a testator/trustor is not sure of the exact status of his inter vivos trust at the time of preparing his will, it could be revoked, thusly—

and (as applicable)

I specifically revoke that Inter Vivos Trust dated December 15, 2005 executed at Reno, Nevada.

Particular care must be taken to revoke only revocable trusts. There are also *irrevocable* trusts; they cannot be undone. On point is the classical "ILIT trap" [Irrevocable Life Insurance Trust]. The ILIT is an institutional gold mine for financial counselors and their legal staffs. Modest-wealth persons are enticed to commit very large annual premiums — $30,000, $50,000, $100,000, or more. If the premium money runs out before death, trying to recover the money by revocation in a will raises soundness-of-mind challenges.

Trust Titling Options

Because of the long-term testamentary nature of a trust, trusts tend to be more complicated than wills. There is also confusion over whether a trust is revocable or irrevocable. Consequently, trust titling is not as straightforward as a will. Here, we are addressing only revocable or living trusts.

For continuity of illustration purposes, our fictitious trustor is John Quincy Jones. For the moment, consider that he is a solo trustor. The title caption to his trust could be any of these variants:

DECLARATION OF LIVING TRUST
BY
JOHN QUINCY JONES

or,

DECLARATION OF INTER VIVOS TRUST
BY . . .

or,

DECLARATION OF REVOCABLE TRUST
BY . . .

or,

DECLARATION OF TRUST
BY . . .

or some other title with the word "declaration" in it. The term *declaration* is a formal statement that carries the same contractual impact after death as "Last Will and Testament." Incidentally, the word "by" means: *created by*.

The common practice these days when creating a living trust is to have the trustor make a will first. Via the will, the trustor/testator declares his mental faculties and revocation clauses similarly as set forth above. This saves repeating these matters in the preamble of the trust, while simultaneously clearing out the low-valued items of the decedent's estate (by direct bequests) before transferring the major property of value to the trust. We call this arrangement a "pots and pans" will. It enables each testator/trustor to rid the clutter and miscellany from that person's trust estate. Unfortunately, the instructions for doing so are not clear and specific. The impression given is that everything, pots and pans included, goes to the trust.

In the case of married testators/trustors, the residual trust estate of each individual trustor is conjoined into a *family trust* after each trustor dies. This is the quite common practice among professional trust preparers. They prepare the family trust instrument as two separate trusts within a common trust. This way, each spouse can prescribe his or her own property distribution intentions, independently of the other. In the end, whatever property is left over is combined into one family trust for ongoing distributions to heirs and kin. A depiction of the key features of a conjoined trust is presented in Figure 2.2. While one trustor is still living, the decedent trustor's instructions are honored in full.

A conjoined trust is truly a humane and practical convenience. It looks ahead in time to those circumstances when one or both spouses, before death, may become senile, blind, deaf, disabled, or develop Alzheimer's disease. The central idea behind any trust estate is to generate sufficient income to support each trustor until the very end.

With Figure 2.2 and the above commentary in mind, how would the common trust of John Quincy and Mary Jane Jones be appropriately titled?

One version could be—

DECLARATION OF JONES FAMILY TRUST
BY
JOHN QUINCY JONES & MARY JANE JONES

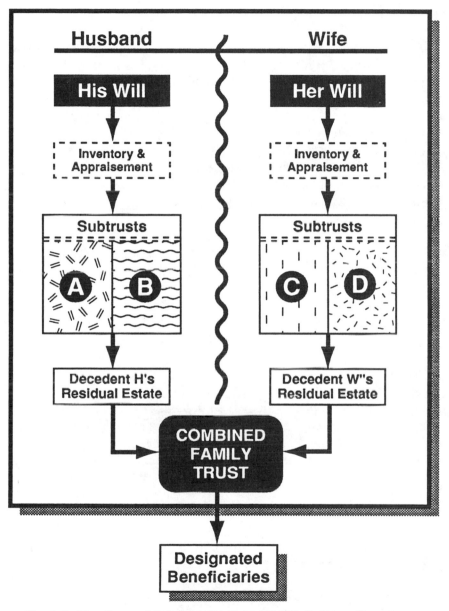

Fig. 2.2 - The General Scheme of a Spousal Family Trust Document

or whatever other wording that is appropriate. Citing the names of both spouses in full makes it clear which family trust is created.

Example Preamble by Trustor(s)

The preamble wording in a trust instrument is much more expressive of intent than that in a will. This is because a trust is a long-term contract. Consequently, each state's trust law requires at least an introductory reference to—

(1) intention to create,
(2) designation of trust property,
(3) statement of trust purpose,
(4) designation of beneficiaries, and
(5) appointment of trustee(s).

These elements should be mentioned early on in the trust instrument. Accordingly, for illustration purposes, we continue with trustors John and Mary, and their Family Trust. The preamble wording of their trust might read as—

JOHN QUINCY JONES, Husband, and MARY JANE JONES, Wife, declare that by this agreement they hereby create the JONES FAMILY TRUST.

Purpose of Trust
The purpose of the Trust is to provide for the protection and management of the Trustors' assets during their lifetimes and to provide for the orderly disposition of the residual assets of the Trust upon the deaths of the Trustors, without any supervision by the Court.

Trust Estate
All of the property described in Schedule A attached to this instrument, and any other property that may hereafter be subject to this Trust, shall constitute the "Trust estate." It shall be held, administered, and distributed in accordance with this instrument. Any property (community, quasi-community, or separate) transferred to the Trust shall retain its initial character after its transfer.

And so on. The beneficiaries of the trust are named, and their relationship to the trustors is stated. The appointment of an initial trustee (or co-trustees) is named; one or more successor trustees also are named. Should a vacancy in trusteeship occur, instructions should be given for appointing a new trustee to fill the vacancy.

Signaturizing & Witnessing

The purpose of preamble wording is to declare the gratuitous intent and soundness of mind of the property owner. At some point in its preparatory time, a testamentary instrument must close. The closing paragraph thereof provides opportunity to further reaffirm the mental state of the testator or trustor.

In the case of a **will**, the testator signs his testament in the presence of at least two witnesses. Without the testator realizing it, the witnesses are supposed to engage the testator in some innocuous conversation about "affairs of state" (whatever that might entail). By doing so, in the event that the will is challenged after the testator's death, one or both witnesses can testify as to its validity.

And so, the closing paragraph of a will might read—

IN WITNESS WHEREOF, I have hereto set my hand this 31st day of January, 2004.

(Signature of testator)
JOHN QUINCY JONES

The foregoing document consisting of 5 pages, including this page, was on the date thereof by JOHN QUINCY JONES, the maker thereof, signed in our presence and in the presence of each of us, and at the time of subscribing said document he declared that it was his Last Will and Testament, and at his request and in his presence and in the presence of each other, we have subscribed our names as witnesses thereto.

(Signature of witness)   *Residing at* _____

_____

(Signature of witness)   *Residing at*_____

_____

In the case of a trust, not only does the trustor sign, the initial trustee also signs. The reason for both trustor and trustee signing is that a trust is a contractual agreement to be conducted over an extended period of time. This means two signatures: one by the property owner and one by the fiduciary of the trust estate. In the case of a family trust, there would be four signatures: two trustors and two trustees. The second trustee could be a co-trustee or a successor trustee who is named in the trust instrument.

Accordingly, the closing paragraph of a trust agreement might read straightforwardly as—

The Trustors hereby grant and assign the property listed on the attached Schedule A to the Trustee, and the Trustee hereby acknowledges acceptance of the property IN TRUST upon the terms and conditions herein stated.

IN WITNESS WHEREOF, the Trustors and Trustees have executed this Agreement this 31st day of January, 2004.

/s/_____ *JOHN QUINCY JONES* *Trustor*	/s/___(Initial Trustee)_____ _____(Printed name)_____ *Trustee*
/s/_____ *MARY JANE JONES* *Trustor*	/s/ (Co- or Successor Trustee)___ (Printed name) *Trustee*

Because of the contractual nature of a trust, the witnessing is done by a **Notary Public**. A Notary Public is an officer of the state where he/she is commissioned. An official seal signifies the notary's authority to administer oaths and to authenticate documents. The notary personally meets with each trustor and each trustee, and assures himself (on the basis of satisfactory evidence) that each indeed is the person that each claims to be. Upon this, the notary signs, dates, and affixes his/her Official Seal.

3

FEATURES OF A WILL

A Will Is A Testamentary Document You Can Prepare On Your Own. It Is A "Variable Contingency Plan" Should A Fatal Disaster Occur Before Retirement. It Requires Arrangement Into "Subject Specific" Paragraphs Where Each Intended Distributee Is Identified In Terms Of His Or Her Portions Of Property In Kind, In Dollars, Or In Percentages Of Your Net Estate. For Married Couples, Separate Wills Provide More Property Distribution Flexibity. As Your Family Status And Property Status Change, So, Too, Should Your Will Change. For Basic Content Wording, STATUTORY WILL FORMS Are Available In Many States To Help You Get Started.

An ordinary will comprises between three and five pages of testamentary text. It is not a complicated affair, once you realize that it has a specific purpose that only you as a property owner and, possibly, as a parent of minor children, can direct. Whatever your directions may be, they can be executed only after your death, and even then, only once. Except when you appoint a guardian for minor children and a custodian for their funds, there are no ongoing distributions of assets after your death.

Rarely does a person under age 25 have a will. There is really no need to. As a single person with property of value less than $100,000, a will can be avoided altogether. There are other testamentary arrangements that a single person can pursue.

It is not until one is married, and the first child is born, that a will becomes prudent and necessary. At this stage, you have the deaths of two adult persons to think about: you and your spouse. You also have to think about the possibility of simultaneous deaths and the potential orphaning of one or more minor children. With or without property of value, providing for minors (after parental deaths) is perhaps the greatest tribute to the wisdom of a will.

Accordingly, in this chapter, we want to familiarize you with the basic contents of a will, how it is organized, how you can write your will to minimize the need for probate, and how you can change your will from time to time as circumstances warrant. The greatest virtue of a will is its relative simplicity. This means that you can — and should — prepare it on your own. For this purpose, there are what are called: *statutory will forms* that you can use.

Do not confuse an ordinary will with a Durable Power of Attorney (for business decisions or for health care) which is sometimes termed a "living will." The *duration* aspect of a durable power takes effect upon the onset of mental incapacity and "endures" only up to the point of death. An ordinary will **starts** at time of death.

Purpose & Contents

Many persons put off and never get around to preparing their wills. They do so because of uncertainty at to what the purpose is and what information is to be included. By and large, though, most persons postpone making a will for one simple reason. They dread the thought of death. They are right. Very few persons enjoy such thoughts, regardless of their age.

A better way is to think of a will as a temporary contingency plan in the event of some fatal unforeseen. It is "temporary" because it can be changed many times during your productive years of life. As long as a will's primary purpose is met (providing for surviving spouse and minor children, if any), there is no limit to the number of changes that can be made.

In Chapter 2, we've already told you about two basic requirements of a solid will. These are your state of mind and your closing signature in the presence of two witnesses. Between this opening and closing is where you state your position and intentions regarding the distribution of your property. You need only do this in clear factual terms that are as nearly self-interpretive as possible. Try to avoid wordiness and ambiguity.

Without details at this point, we list as follows the basic contents of any ordinary will:

1. Revocation clause
2. Family status
3. Appointment of executor
4. Powers of executor
5. Nature of property
6. Principal distributee(s)
7. Successor distributee(s)
8. Appointment of guardian
9. Appointment of custodian
10. Disinheritance clause

A thumbnail description of each of these content items is presented in Figure 3.1. A "distributee" is a designated recipient of *your* property only. A "guardian" is one who oversees the raising of your minor children until legal age (18 in California). A "custodian" is one who manages your property for the health, support, maintenance, and education of your children until a specified age (no later than 25 in California).

The content listing in Figure 3.1 is not exclusive. Other items of importance to you as the testator can be added. For example, if you want a particular parcel of property sold, say so. If a particular debtor owes you money, and you've had difficulty collecting it over the years, spell it out. If you've made tax accountable gifts to close family members while alive, list them. If you wish to distribute property unequally to adult children, indicate the degree of inequality with different percentages. If you own or co-own a small business in which you are the primary "mover and shaker," indicate whether the business should be continued, liquidated, or sold. If there are parents, uncles, aunts, cousins, nieces, or nephews who have financial need, and you can help them, spell out their full names, and indicate specifically what you want them to have: items in kind, dollar amounts, or percentage amounts.

Construction & Interpretation

For good reason, a will is written in discreet subject-specific paragraphs. The term "subject-specific" means one class of property or one class of distributee at a time. This is so that if one paragraph is found to be ambiguous or potentially invalid, it will not restrict carrying out your intentions in other paragraphs. You do not want to risk invalidating your entire will for some ambiguity of interpretation that might occur without your knowledge, long after your death.

¶	Subject Matter	Specific Focus
1	Revocation	To clear away all prior testamentary declarations that may have been made.
2	Family Status	Identification of spouse, children, and others to whom distribution intended.
3	Executor Name(s)	The person(s) you want to carry out the intentions you prescribe.
4	Powers of Executor	Legal powers re sole discretion, sale of realty, settling estate, without bond.
5	Nature of Property	Whether real, tangible, intangible, or personal; owner & co-owners thereof.
6	Primary Distributees	Living persons who are to get the bulk of your estate: $ or %.
7	Successor Distributees	Survivors of those above; if none, executor to reproportion the property.
8	Guardian	For person(s) of minor children under age 18; health, support, education.
9	Custodian	For property of any child under age 25; dole out money to guardian and others.
10	Disinheritance	Via commonly worded "$1 clause" to thwart would-be troublemakers.

Fig. 3.1 - Brief Description of Paragraphic Contents of an Ordinary Will

In a will, you indicate each subject-specific paragraph with capital letters: FIRST, SECOND, THIRD, . . . TENTH (or whatever is last). Because of the comparative shortness of a will (3 to 5 pages), there is no need to subtitle each paragraph. Simply indicate the subject matter in the first sentence of each paragraph. There may be subparagraphs — (a), (b), (c), etc. — within one or more of your principal paragraphs.

Almost any will, no matter how complex your affairs may be, can be organized into multiple separate paragraphs functionally distinct from each other. There is no particular order to your paragraphic writings. However, a natural flow evolves from your basic wishes towards your spouse, children, kin, and other close persons, whether family members or not.

As for interpreting any ambiguous wording or intent in a will paragraph, probate law controls. In those wills where there are substantial property holdings and a substantial number of distributees, a separate paragraph is added to expressly indicate which state law, which division, and which part thereof shall be consulted. For example, in California, its probate law has a Division 11: *Construction of Wills, Trusts, and Other Instruments*, of which Part I thereof is titled: *Rules for Interpretation of Instruments*. An informed testator can cite (or refer to) any one or more of the 30 interpretive sections in CPC Division 11, Part 1. When doing so, however, be aware that the terminology used applies not only to wills, but also to "trusts and other instruments."

Purely for instructional purposes, we have selected the three following citations:

CPC § 21102: *Intention of transferor as controlling.*

*The **intention** of the transferor as expressed in this instrument controls the legal effect of the dispositions made in the instrument.*

CPC § 21107: *Conversion of real property into money.*

*If an instrument directs the conversion of real property into money at the transferor's death, the property and its proceeds **shall be deemed personal property** from the time of the transferor's death.*

CPC § 21120: *Interpretation of words to give every expression some effect.*

Preference is to be given to an interpretation that will give every expression some effect . . . rather than one that will result in an intestacy.

The term "instrument" refers to a will, trust, deed (title to real property), gift, or other testamentary-type writing. The term "transferor" refers to a testator, trustor, owner, donor, or other person who transfers property gratuitously to another person or persons, or to a charitable cause.

Please reread the second citation above, namely: CPC § 21107. We have a side commentary to make. By your directing that one or more expressly-identified parcels of real property be sold upon your demise, you are converting said property into personal property, called: *money*. Under the right circumstances, money transfers often can be treated as nonprobative assets. This is because, when real property is sold, a condition for passing clear title to the buyer is that all mortgages, liens, debts, expenses, taxes, and professional fees be paid from its gross sale proceeds. This is somewhat akin to the probative process itself. There is a hint here that perhaps you should take note of.

Joint Wills: No-No

The experience of ordinary adult life generally includes at one time or another the institution of marriage. So common is this marital association that the concept of "jointness" is prevalent in our society. This is especially true in matters of income tax returns, property deeds, bank accounts, charge cards, and so on.

Couples who have been married 10, 20, 30 years or so come to think of themselves as one and the same person. Therefore, the desire to prepare a joint will is a natural and logical consequence of their durable marriage.

Though there is nothing improper in a joint will, it is extremely cumbersome to execute. What we have is a single testamentary instrument that binds two persons to its terms. The chief disadvantage of doing so is that it obscures the testamentary capacity of the surviving spouse. The plausible argument can be posed that each spouse had undue influence on the other. Consequently, in virtually every case of a joint will, *probate is required* when the first spouse dies. This is particularly so if the joint will includes beneficiaries other than the surviving spouse, where one or more of the beneficiaries are not the blood-line heir(s) of the surviving spouse. The heir-kin problems of divorce and remarriage come to mind. There also could be problems with "adoptees-in-law."

The probate presumption is that a joint will was entered into pursuant to some oral agreement between the two spouses. The interpretive effect is to prevent the surviving spouse from changing or revoking any of the will terms. In other words, it is presumed that both spouses entered into a binding pre-death contract that cannot be broken after the death of the first spouse. Where there is a gap of several to many years between the two deaths, a joint will can impose severe hardship on the surviving spouse.

The gist of the point being made is that a joint will, or any of its variants, is a "No-No." It is highly questionable on physical grounds that two minds are one and the same, even though at the time of preparing the will, they may think alike. But the moment one spouse is deceased, there are no longer two minds to think alike. Thus, clearly, the surviving spouse's testamentary capacity and right of revocation has been jeopardized. Was the surviving joint will signer subjected to any undue influence by the decedent spouse?

Therefore, each spouse should prepare his/her own will in a complete and separate document from the other. The two wills can be prepared at the same time, and even exactly mirror each other. The result becomes two "mirror wills" instead of one joint will. Many of the same objectives of a joint will can be accomplished by mirror wills, with much greater flexibility.

Simultaneous Deaths

An even stronger argument against joint wills is the possibility of simultaneous — or near-simultaneous — deaths of husband and wife. Spousal wills generally anticipate that one or the other will be the surviving spouse. In such event, the surviving spouse "gets everything" . . . virtually. So, what happens if there's a fatal car accident, plane crash, wildfire, tornado, flood, or other calamity where both spouses perish?

Answer: This is where the simultaneous-death statute of state law comes into play. Said law prevails unless some other clear provison is stated in each spouse's separate will.

In California, the siultaneous death law is set forth in CPC § 220: *Disposition of property; insufficient evidence of survivorship.* In its most pertinent part, this law reads—

If the title to property or the devolution [passing down] *of property depends upon priority of death and it cannot be established by clear and convincing evidence that one of the persons survived the other,* ***the property of each person*** *shall be administered . . . as if that person had survived the other.*

The net effect of CPC § 220 is that each spouse's will is read as though each spouse had predeceased the other. As a result, all surviving spouse clauses are bypassed. Then, the next person in line (as designated in each separate will) takes his or her proper share of each decedent's property. A depiction of this consequence is presented in Figure 3.2.

If there is no simultaneous-death recognition in each spouse's will, and simultaneous — or near-simultaneous — death indeed occurs, probate proceedings are required. Rather than allowing this to happen, a limited-period common-disaster clause should be set forth. A "limited period" is a reasonable length of time (30, 60, 90 days or so) to sort out the survivorability aspects of a common disaster. Otherwise, simultaneous deaths are construed to mean within five days of each other.

For example, testator JOHN with wife MARY and three children might state:

TWELFTH

In the event that my wife, MARY, should not survive me more than 30 days, OR in the event that MARY and I shoud perish in a common disaster, OR in the event that MARY should predecease me, then all of my net estate, in kind or value, shall be distributed equally among my three children, DAVID, JANE, and JOSEPH.

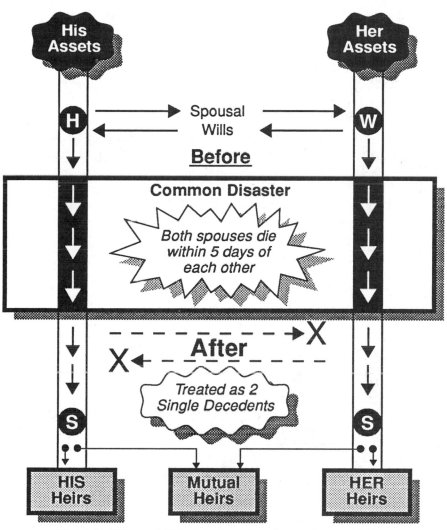

Fig. 3.2 - Effect of Simultaneous Deaths on Spousal Wills

Percentages or Dollars?

The foregoing distributive instruction: "all of my net estate, in kind or value, shall be distributed equally among . . ." can cause much unintended ambiguity. Legitimate questions can be raised as to the meaning of: (1) net estate, (2) in kind or value, and (3) equally among. These are commonly used terms in every will. Without clarification, they often give rise to probate proceedings unnecessarily.

The term "net estate" generally means whatever is left over AFTER all other matters are addressed. Among these *other matters* are probate proceedings (if any), taxes of all kinds (income, property, employment, death, etc.), claims by the decedent against others, debts of the decedent, mortgages outstanding, lawsuits in process, administrative expenses, professional fees, and other related matters. For example, suppose that elsewhere in his will, JOHN (the testator above) made a pecuniary (monetary) bequest of $50,000 to his mother and another such bequest of $25,000 to his sister. That's a total of $75,000 in pecuniary bequests. Unless specific provisions were made to the contrary, these amounts would be paid before the net estate is available for distribution to JOHN's three children.

Re the term "in kind or value," suppose that JOHN wanted the family's grand piano to go to JANE (a pianist). This would be a distribution "in kind." But is this part of her 33 1/3% "equally among"? If so, the piano would have to be market valued and subtracted from JANE's 33 1/3% amount. If not, JOHN should say so, in a separate paragraph for distributions in kind.

Whenever you use common words like "equally," it is best to spell out your intentions in precise percentages. This way you can "round the numbers" . . . and designate the distributions *unequally*. All distributions to children do not have to be equal. When children are of different ages and sex, each has different financial needs (health, education, support). However, if all are mature adults (age 35 or so), equally may be indicated. Example distributions to the three children above could be—

	Equally	Unequally
DAVID	33.33%	20.00%
JANE	33.34%	35.00%
JOSEPH	33.33%	45.00%
	100.00%	100.00%

To avoid potential ambiguities, we urge formulating your distributive intentions in the functional groupings presented in Figure 3.3. A will, in and of itself, signifies the complete distribution of *all* your property after your demise. The best way to do this is to rid your estate of distributions in kind, pecuniary bequests, and obligations of the decedent *before* computing your net distributable estate.

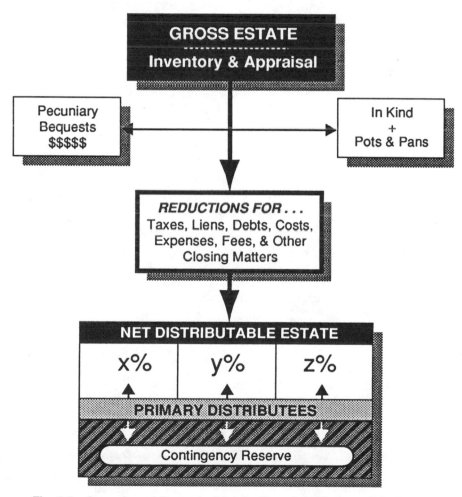

GROSS ESTATE
- - - - - - - - - - - - - - - - - -
Inventory & Appraisal

Pecuniary
Bequests
$$$$$

In Kind
+
Pots & Pans

REDUCTIONS FOR . . .
Taxes, Liens, Debts, Costs,
Expenses, Fees, & Other
Closing Matters

NET DISTRIBUTABLE ESTATE

| x% | y% | z% |

PRIMARY DISTRIBUTEES

Contingency Reserve

Fig. 3.3 - Grouping of Property Distributions for Closing a Will Estate

The Disinheritance Clause

Except for a surviving spouse and minor children, if any, a testator can disinherit any and all of his natural heirs. It is not necessary that he have any particular reason for doing so. A testator is free — after taxes, debts, and expenses — to dispose of as much or as little of his estate to his heirs as he sees fit. He is under no obligation to dispose of it equally, nor is he required to dispose of it according to some percentage formula. Only in the case of intestate succession are inherited portions fixed by law.

In a practical world, squabbling among heirs over a deceased person's estate is quite common. In the process, some surprise person will come out of the woodwork to claim a financial interest in your estate. It could be an ex-spouse, a distant nephew, or an out-of-wedlock child (now an adult).

The best way to protect your estate against surprise claimants is to include a *disinheritance clause*. This inclusion in your will is also known as "the $1 clause." Such a clause has been challenged many times and found to be valid. Its wording, however, must be clear and specific. If so, it legally shuts out those who would try to make trouble for your expressly designated distributees. Its greatest impact is when it is your very last declaratory statement . . . just before IN WITNESS WHEREOF. After your burial or cremation, it is customary to read the will to all heirs and distributees named therein. The disinheritance clause should leave no doubt in their minds what you intended.

Suppose, for example, that JOHN QUINCY JONES (our fictitious testator) wants to specifically exclude his ex-spouse, MARGARET ANN (MOOREHEAD) JONES, and all unknown others. He would declare as follows:

I have intentionally and with full knowledge omitted to provide herein for my former wife, MARGARET ANN (MOOREHEAD) JONES. If MARGARET, or any person or persons, other than those provided for herein, should prove a right to participate in the distribution of my estate, to each and all of such person or persons proving a right to so participate, I give, devise, and bequeath the sum of One dollar ($1.00) only.

It is extremely difficult — almost impossible — to crack this $1 clause and prove it invalid. Any claimant not expressly named in the will has the sole burden of doing so. Even if proof is sustained, the award is "One dollar ($1.00) only."

Holographic Wills

The term "holo" means *whole*; "graphic" means *written*. Hence, a holographic will is one which is written in its entirety in the handwriting of the testator. It is signed and dated. It is not witnessed, nor is it notarized.

To be valid, *every word* of a holographic will must be in the handwriting of the testator. It cannot be part typed and part handwritten. It cannot be on letterhead; no ink-pad stampings on it are allowed. Only blank paper can be used and the entire document from start to finish must be legibly handwritten. Because handwritten words can be misread, names can be misspelled, and intentions can be misinterpreted, holographic wills are seldom recognized. If there are substantial assets and two or more heirs are designated, such wills invite endless litigation and haggling.

Such wills are most commonly recognized when written by testators living in isolated and remote areas, in combat zones, and in nursing homes. One is not disenfranchised of his right to a will just because of his place of living or of the small value of his assets. Handwritten wills are primarily the domain of "small estates" (under $100,000 or so).

Holographic wills are useful as temporary dispositions of property pending more formal typing of a witnessed will. If one is in an extended travel status, or in the process of moving from one residence to another county, state, or country, the holographic will is an excellent expedient. If one already has a computer printed will, a holographic statement can be regarded as a temporary codicil (amendment) to that will.

There is one positive and highly recommended use of the holographic concept. It is ideal for the testamentary disposition of purely personal items and effects. For example, personal clothing, family heirlooms, homey artifacts, picture albums, out-of-style jewelry, nonmarketable antiques, and other such items can be conveniently disposed of via a holographic addendum to a printed will. These items have negligible market value for death taxation purposes. They are identified merely as "incidental personal effects." One can dispose of them legitimately in a separate handwritten testament.

Statutory Will Forms

Some states, California among them, have authorized the use of statutory wills. These are preprinted forms of the fill-in-the-blanks type. Each box and blank line is accompanied by self-guiding instructions. After a shorter preprinted paragraphic statement of your intentions, you are instructed to—

Select one choice only and sign in the box after your choice.

All the unsigned boxes are void. The forms (in those states where authorized) can be purchased in office supply and stationery stores that sell legal forms.

The will form is headed generally as follows:

CALIFORNIA STATUTORY WILL OF

Print Your Full Name

This is my Will. I revoke all prior Wills and codicils.

This heading is followed by subheaded paragraphs (with blank lines and boxes) such as—

- Specific Gift of Personal Residence
- Specific Gift of Automobiles, Household and Personal Effects
- Specific Gifts of Cash
- Balance of My Assets
- Guardian of the Child's Person under Age 18
- Custodian for Property of Persons under Age 25
- Choice for Executor

• Is a Bond Required (for the executor)?

Where pertinent, there are four distributee choices offered to a testator. These choices are—

a. **Choice One** — *All to my spouse, if my spouse survives me; otherwise to my children and the descendants of my children who survive me.*

b. **Choice Two** — *Nothing to my spouse; all to my children and the descendants of my children who survive me.*

c. **Choice Three** — *All to the following person if he or she survives me:*

_____

d. **Choice Four** — *Equally among the following persons who survive me:*

_____

_____

_____

The reason for choice options, blank lines, and blank boxes (as diagrammed in Figure 3.4) is that one statutory form "fits all estates." This is not exactly true, of course. Still, a statutory will does fit many ordinary family situations. Therefore, we cannot overstress the instructional importance of procuring such a will form on your own. Even if you do not actually fill it out, it becomes an invaluable reference for what you can do, and cannot do, on your own.

Attorney Not Necessary

There is a particular reason for urging you to procure a copy of the statutory will form for your state of domicile. The statutory

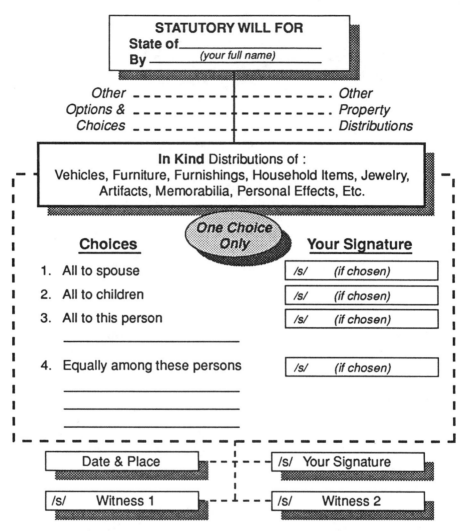

Fig. 3.4 - Sample of Blank Lines & Boxes in Statutory Will Form

form can be used as an outline for preparing your own will by typewriter or computer. You can omit the blank lines and boxes that do not apply to you. You can read the questions and answers that accompany the form, and reformulate your distributive intentions in your own words. No attorney is necessary for this.

The *writing* of a will comes under the jurisdiction of no court in the United States. There is no federal law, and no state law, that requires an attorney for the preparation of a will. Therefore, each individual is free to write his own will as he sees fit, or to seek suggestions from attorneys and nonattorneys alike. Much depends on each individual's own preferences.

Our position is that, if you are under age 55 with a young and growing family, you'll be changing your will many times before reaching your retirement years. You don't want to be running to an attorney for every little change in your family and property status. Set your will up on your computer, print it out, and get it witnessed. When you make a change, print it out again and get it witnessed again. The idea is that, until you really get into your retirement years, a will is strictly a *contingency plan*. It is a testamentary document to have on hand, should some fatal disaster occur. It is not an "estate plan" in the sense that would apply to an elderly person in his post-retirement years.

Prudence suggests that if you have complicated property affairs (multiple real estate holdings; $1,000,000 or more in financial accounts), disharmonious spousal interests, or mixed heirs and kin (due to divorce and remarriage), a knowledgeable attorney should be sought. Even so, caution should prevail when engaging any attorney. Too often, attorneys make matters worse. They love controversy and the stretching of your pockets. They tend to intimidate rather than inform. So try to simplify your affairs as much as possible on your own.

For helping you simplify affairs, the California statutory-will form carries the instruction that—

You should make and sign a new Will if you marry or divorce after signing this Will. Divorce or annulment automatically cancels all property stated to pass to a former husband or wife under this Will, and revokes the designation of a former spouse as executor, custodian, or guardian. You should sign a new Will when you have more children, or if your spouse or child dies. You may want to change your Will if there is a large change in the value of your assets.

Do you really want to pay an attorney to tell you this, or can you not follow this instruction on your own?

Nonprobate Transfers

Even a statutory will form gives you some hint on the effect of a will on probative and nonprobative transfers. For example, the California form is prefaced by a number of questions and answers, a few of which touch on the subject of probate. Two such preprinted questions (and their answers) are—

Q. *Does a Will avoid probate?*

A. *No. With or without a Will, assets in your name alone usually go through the court probate process. The court's first job is to determine if your Will is valid.*

Right away you have two hints. Property in "your name alone" requires probate . . . "usually." If property is in your name and one or more others, probate is not required (except where there is conflict among the surviving owners). The term "usually" is meant to include estates whose value exceeds $100,000. For smaller estates, the affidavit procedure applies; hence, no probate.

Q. *Do all assets go through probate?*

A. *No. Money in a joint tenancy bank account automatically belongs to the other named owner without probate. If your spouse or child is on the deed to your house as a joint tenant, the house automatically passes to him or her. Life insurance and retirement plan benefits may pass directly to the named beneficiary. A Will does not necessarily control how these types of nonprobate assets pass at your death.*

The point we are getting at is that there are such matters as nonprobate *transfers* and nonprobate *assets*. A nonprobate "transfer" includes, in addition to your own name, someone else's name on your property or financial account. A nonprobate "asset" is an item such as registered vehicle, household furniture and furnishings, and personal clothing and effects which are not ordinarily probate eligible whatsoever.

4

FEATURES OF A TRUST

Family Trusts Are Created Under State Law Where The Husband And Wife Trustors Reside. Thereupon, The "Trust Instrument" Becomes A CONTRACTUAL AGREEMENT Between Trustors And Trustees For The Distribution Of Property, Gratuitously, To One Or More Beneficiaries. Only "Property Of Value" Is Assigned To The Trust. All Other "Pots And Pans" And Small Direct Bequests Are Disposed Of Via Pretrust Wills. Where There Are Numerous Children And Grandchildren Living When The First Trustor Dies, The Distributive Clauses Become Obfuscating And Complex. So, Too, Does The 21-Year Termination Rule Against Perpetuating A Trust.

Unlike a decedent's estate which is automatic upon death, a trust is not a natural occurrence. It has to be intentionally created. A trust is created under state law and, as such, it becomes a legal entity thereof. As a legal entity, a trust instrument tends to be lengthy and obfuscating (obscure and unclear). For an ordinary family trust, the instrument can easily run between 30 and 50 pages of printed text.

Rarely is a trust instrument prepared by a trustor/trustee himself or herself. Professional preparers — attorneys, mostly — must be employed. Their objective is to formulate a contractual arrangement between trustors and trustees with respect to the distribution of designated trust property. Where there is a husband trustor and a wife trustor for the same trust property, numerous distribution contingencies have to be thought through. This is because at time of preparation there can be no presumption as to which spouse will predecease the other. The result is that family trusts tend to be a *joint* instrument by both the husband and the wife.

In this chapter, we want to address family living trusts only. In doing so, we intentionally bypass all discussion of special-purpose trusts and all forms of abusive trusts for tax avoidance purposes. While a family trust (when property "funded") may indeed avoid probate, it cannot avoid tax which is otherwise applicable. There is much confusion over the distinction between probative and taxation matters. So much so that we have reserved two separate chapters — Chapters 10 and 11, respectively — to discuss each of these processes in depth.

Meanwhile, there is a whole domain of family trust features that you should know about. Having a trust for the sake of simply having a trust is not what we have in mind. For the serious-minded trustor, a trust can be an invaluable aid for distributing property gratuitously over extended periods of time after the second trustor's death. By now you should know that a "trustor" is one who owns property and who transfers it into trust for distribution to others by someone called a "trustee." Hence, there is creation of a *contract* between trustor and trustee. What makes this contract enforceable after death are the provisions of state law.

State Law Provisions

Every state where a potential trustor resides has its own trust law. Said law is found in the Probate Code for that state. You do not have to be an attorney to access the probate code for your state. Visit the legal section of your local public library, or visit the county law library nearest you. County law libraries are tax-exempt entities. As such, they must allow public access if they wish to continue their tax-exempt status. Browse through the trust law division looking for sections that attract your attention in a common sense way. If you are intrigued by a particular section, photocopy it for perusal later. Or search your state's website or the law library's website for the probate code division titled: *Trust Law*.

As we have done previously, we will cite specific excerpts from the California Probate Code [CPC] in order to illustrate what a trust is all about. In particular, we cite from Part 2 of California's trust law which is titled: *Creation, Validity, Modification, and Termination of Trusts*. A few excerpts from the 6,000-word treatise will help you identify with the key characteristics of a valid trust. Other states have similar trust validity rules.

Accordingly, our selected excerpts (with the CPC section numbers) are:

1. *A trust is created only if the settlor* [trustor] *properly manifests an intention to create a trust.* [§ 15201]

2. *A trust is created only if there is trust property.* [§ 15202]

3. *A trust may be created for any purpose that is not illegal or against public policy.* [§ 15203]

4. *A trust . . . is created only if there is a beneficiary. This requirement is satisfied if the trust instrument provides for either of the following:*

   (a) A beneficiary or class of beneficiaries that is ascertainable with reasonably certainty or that is sufficiently described so it can be determined that some person meets the description or is within the class.

   (b) A grant of a power to the trustee or some other person to select the beneficiaries based on a standard or in the discretion of the trustee or other person. [§ 15205]

5. *If the trust instrument provides that a beneficiary's interest in income is not subject to voluntary or involuntary transfer, the beneficiary's interest in income under the trust may not be transferred and is not subject to enforcement of a money judgment until paid to the beneficiary.* [§ 15300]

6. *If the trust instrument provides that a beneficiary's interest in principal* [corpus] *is not subject to voluntary or involuntary transfer, the beneficiary's interest in principal*

may not be transferred and is not subject to enforcement of a money judgment until paid to the beneficiary. [§ 15301]

7. *Unless a trust instrument is expressly made irrevocable by the trust instrument, the trust is revocable by the settlor* [trustor]. *This applies only where the settlor is domiciled in this state when the trust is created, where the trust instrument is executed in this state, or where the trust instrument provides that the law of this state governs the trust.* [§ 15400]

8. *If all beneficiaries of an irrevocable trust consent, they may compel modification or termination of the trust upon petition to the* [probate] *court.* [§ 15403]

9. *A trust terminates when any of the following occurs:*

   (a)   The term of the trust expires.
   (b)   The trust purpose is fulfilled.
   (c)   The trust purpose becomes unlawful.
   (d)   The trust purpose becomes impossible to fulfill.
   (e)   The trust is revoked. [§ 15407]

Manifestation of Intent

As you can see in the citations above, the first required feature of a trust is that there be specific creational intent. How does one manifest this intent? Answer: With clearly stated preamble wording, citing the purpose of the trust.

Every trust instrument starts with preamble wording that states the names of the trustors, the initial trustees, and the name and date of creation of the family trust. The particular words used follow the format and style of the trust preparer's own choosing. There is an air of contractual formality, which indeed there should be. The document is formally labeled—

DECLARATION OF TRUST

For example, using purely fictitious names, the preamble wording might read as—

JOHN J. JONES, Husband, and MARY M. JONES, wife, called the "Trustors" and the "Trustees" depending on the context, declare that by this Agreement they hereby create the JONES FAMILY TRUST, which is entered into on such date as is set forth hereinafter.

The above wording may be followed by a subheading, such as: *Purpose of Trust.* Example wording could be—

The purpose of the Trust is to provide for the protection and management of the Trustors' assets during their joint lifetimes and to provide for the orderly disposition of assets of the Trust upon the death of the Trustors without any supervision by the Court.

The phrase "without any supervision by the Court" clearly expresses the intent to avoid probate when conveying property after the deaths of the joint trustors. The term "by the Court" means: by the Probate Court having jurisdiction at the time and place where the trust was executed. This intention to avoid probate, however, does not preempt the Court from its jurisdiction when bona fide disputes arise over ambiguities in the trust contract itself.

The effective date of a family trust is that on which the contract is preparationally complete, executed, and witnessed. On page 35 or thereabouts, the signatures authenticating the trust contract would appear as—

IN WITNESS WHEREOF, the Trustors and Trustees have executed this Agreement on the ___20th___ day of ___September, 2005___.

/s/_____   /s/_____
       JOHN J. JONES,   *JOHN J. JONES,*
         Trustor   *Trustee*

/s/_____   /s/_____
          MARY M. JONES,   *MARY M. JONES,*
             Trustor   *Trustee*

The signatures are notarized on the same date as that entered above.

> *Editorial Note*: When you see the same name as trustor and trustee, you know that the trust instrument is a revocable document. When you see husband and wife, both as trustors and as trustees, you know that there are **two** revocable trust instruments. When one spouse dies, that spouse's trust instrument becomes irrevocable. When the surviving spouse dies, the two independent trusts combine and become irrevocable. At this point, the family trust is created.

Designation of Trust Property

No trust is created until property of value is transferred into it. The mechanism for designating which property is so transferred is commonly called: *Schedule A*. It is also called the "initial funding schedule." This funding feature, which is simply a listing of property, when called Schedule A (or B, or C, etc.) must not be confused with any similarly alphabetized schedules on a tax return. No trust contract is valid until there is property available that can be drawn upon, to carry out the purpose of the trust. Hence, Schedule A is the first official attachment to a trust instrument following notarization of the trustor's and trustee's signatures.

The funding property is also called the *Trust Estate*. Its introduction into the trust reads along these lines—

> *Property subject to this instrument listed in Schedule A attached and to which title is held in the name of the Trust is referred to as the "Trust Estate." It shall be held, administered, and distributed in accordance with this instrument.*

Schedule A lists each property item or class of property items being transferred into trust. The listing is in general terms with a catchall item for those properties that were overlooked or not in existence when the trust instrument was initially formalized.

For example, Schedule A might list—

1. All Trustors' right, title, and interest in their *personal residence* located at _____.

2. All Trustors' right, title, and interest in that parcel of *rental real property* located at _____.

3. All Trustors' right, title, and interest in each of their *investment accounts* located separately at _____, at _____, and at _____.

4. All Trustors' right, title, and interest in their *unincorporated (or incorporated) business*, including all assets associated therewith, known as _____.

5. All Trustors' right, title, and interest in all real, tangible, intangible, and *personal effects* not otherwise disposed of properly by Will.

Other property not listed in Schedule A, but which is subsequently includible in the trust estate, can be identified in Schedule B as *subsequent funding*. It is seldom possible at the time of trust creation to have the presence of mind and records to freeze in place all intended property. Schedule B allows flexibility to add other property at any time. There also could be, as needed, a Schedule C, Schedule D, Schedule E . . . and so on. Any of these subsequent schedules may delete property from an earlier schedule, and replace it with property of a different type and value. With the proper use and updating of the funding schedules, there is no need to change the trust instrument every time your property holdings change for consumption or for investment purposes.

A "Pots and Pans" Will

It is common practice to precede a trust instrument with what we call a "pots and pans" will. Attorneys call it a "pour-over" will. The idea is to use a pretrust will to rid the trust estate of all garage-sale type items, all personal memorabilia, all personal effects (clothing, furniture, utensils), all nominal value in-kind bequests, and all one-time pecuniary (dollar amount) bequests. The type of ongoing property intended for a trust estate should have **income**-producing capability as well as capital **appreciation** potential. Otherwise, the trustee(s) will be bogged down in legal minutiae when the first trustor dies.

There is a separate pots and pans (pour-over) will for each trustor/testator. The pretrust dispositional intent with respect to personal items could read as follows:

I give all of my jewelry, clothing, household furniture and furnishings, automobiles, tools, sports and recreational equipment, family memorabilia, and other tangible articles of a personal nature to my spouse. If my spouse should not survive me then to my children and grandchildren in such manner as they shall agree. If no amicable agreement can be reached among my children and grandchildren, then such items shall be sold for money and the money transferred to the _____ Family Trust.

Other wording would follow the above to indicate that after an inventory and appraisement had been made, and after all debts, expenses, and taxes had been paid, the residual property of value would comprise the trust estate. The pretrust will would also appoint the executor for the deceased spouse's estate. Specific instructions would be given for accomplishing the initial funding of the trust, as per its Schedule A.

In other general respects, the role of a pretrust will is depicted in Figure 4.1. In said figure, we are trying to emphasize the importance of transferring long-lasting property of value to the trust estate. This is obviously easier to do for estates over $1,000,000 (1 million) than for those of lesser value.

Avoidance of Probate

By far, the most everyday practical feature of a living trust is its capability of avoiding probate. The personal effects and "pots and pans" of a decedent's estate have no probative value in the real world. Probate is a time-consuming and costly procedure.

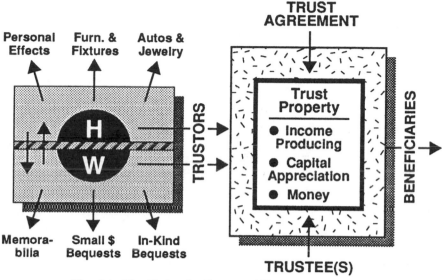

Fig. 4.1 - The Role of a Pretrust Will for Each Trustor

Consequently, probate proceedings target the high-valued property holdings in a decedent's estate, such as: real estate, businesses, and investment accounts.

Probate avoidance rests on one key principle. The prerequisite is that all title to the property in Schedule A be **in the name of the trust** BEFORE either trustor dies. When this is done, the trust legally (on paper) owns the property. In reality, however, only a temporary ownership is created.

The "on paper" aspect permits the trustors, while both are alive, to revoke from the trust any Schedule A item of choice. Revocation is wise where there is a need or desire to sell, exchange, gift, or consume any Schedule A item before one trustor dies. After the first trustor dies, the surviving trustor can only revoke his or her own portion of the trust estate. Only after the second trustor dies does the entire trust estate — Schedules A, B, C, etc. — become irrevocable.

If there are too frequent changes in the funding schedules of trust property, ownership ambiguity could arise. Then probate proceedings could be indicated. This possibility is usually anticipated in one of the contingency clauses in a trust instrument.

The only reliable way to avoid probate is to convey title to property to the trust in a challenge-proof way. This change-of-title feature is particularly important with respect to real estate, whether residential, commercial, agricultural, mining, or other. The transfer procedures necessary are the following:

1. A Quit Claim Deed must be prepared conveying title from the trustors to the trustee.

2. The deed must be properly executed and notarized.

3. The new deed must be recorded in the Recorder's Office for the county and state where the property is physically located.

4. The County Assessor must review the property titling, verify its APN (Assessor's Parcel Number), and determine whether any reassessment of value (for property tax purposes) is required.

After the new title is recorded and assessed (or reassessed), it is a good idea that all property taxes for the assessable year be prepaid in full. This removes any lingering doubt that ownership of the property has been properly conveyed to the trust. Preferably make the payment on a check that correctly displays the name of the trust. For example, the checking account might show ownership as—

The Jones Family Trust
UTA DTD Sept. 20, 2005
John J. Jones & Mary M. Jones
Trustors & Trustees

(The letters "UTA" stand for "Under Trust Agreement"; the letters "DTD" stand for "Dated.")

To give you an example of how the wording on a Quit Claim Deed might appear, we present Figure 4.2. The right-hand portion of the heading accommodates the Recorder's official stamping and documentation numbering. After the conveyance wording, the full legal description of the land (as set forth by the Surveyor) must be

When Recorded Mail To:	OFFICIAL RECORDATION
_____ _____ _____	• Date DOCUMENT # • Time • Fees _____

QUITCLAIM DEED

There is no consideration for this transfer to a revocable living trust for the benefit of TRUSTORS.

We _JOHN J. JONES_ and _MARY M. JONES_ hereby quitclaim to _John J. Jones_ and _Mary M. Jones_ as TRUSTEES of the _JONES FAMILY TRUST_ dated _____ all of their right, title, and interest in that certain real property located in the City of _____ , County of _____ , State of _____ , commonly described as _(full mailing address)_ and legally described as: APN _____ . ALL OF LOT _____

_____

EXCEPTING THEREFROM _____

_____

Dated _____   /s/ _____

Dated _____   /s/ _____

State of _____
County of _____ On _____

before me _____ , Notary Public, personally
appeared _____

WITNESS my hand
and official seal.

Official Seal

/s/ _____

Fig. 4.2 - Document for Transferring Real Property to a Trust

spelled out. Unless specific exceptions are made for underground water, mineral, and oil and gas rights, ownership of real property goes down to the Earth's core.

While Both Trustees Alive

All family living trusts have one obstacle in common. The trust is created while the husband and wife (as co-trustees) are alive. At the time of its creation, in order to make the trust instrument valid, most of the trustors' property has to be transferred to the trust. This means that their property is no longer in their personal names; it is in the name of the trust. Because of this name change aspect, special enabling wording has to be inserted into the trust instrument.

The enabling wording is found on about page 3 (or so) of the 35-page (or so) trust instrument. The section heading is typified by such caption words as—

RIGHTS & POWERS OF TRUSTORS
WHILE BOTH TRUSTORS ARE LIVING

Alternative wording with similar functional purposes may also be used. The basic idea is that, while both trustors are living, they may continue to do with their own property, even though it is no longer in their names, what they would have done with it were it not in trust. This is the revocation feature of all living trusts, reduced to practical terms.

In fact, many husband and wife trustors go about their daily living writing checks, making investments, selling or buying property items, borrowing against their property, and so on. It is only when one trustor dies that the surviving trustor needs to make special note of what he or she thereafter can do with trust property. This causes hesitation and uncertainty in the mind of the surviving trustor, which only worsens with advancing age.

To sidestep the above aspects, many trust preparers suggest that there be a not-in-trust bank account. Or, if such a bank account already exists, continue with it after the trust is created. Preferably, it should be a checking account with the personal joint names of the two spouses thereon. When one spouse trustor dies, an adult child's name can be added. When the second spouse trustor dies, the adult child has immediate access to funds to pay various bills, medical expenses, funeral costs, and other. If the bank account not in trust has less than $100,000 in it, probate would not likely be required

[CPC § 13100]. To portray this particular not-in-trust feature, we present Figure 4.3.

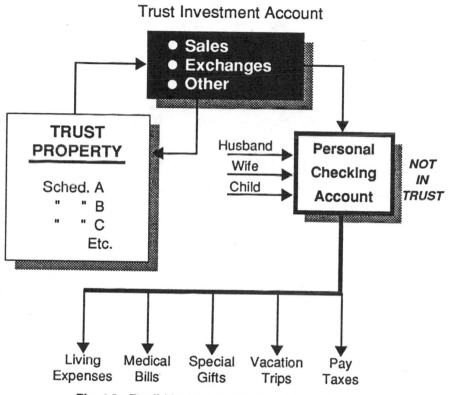

Fig. 4.3 - Flexibility With Not-In-Trust Bank Account

Subtrusts for First Decedent

One of the unavoidable complications of a family trust is the need for designating subtrusts. A "subtrust" is not really a separate trust of its own. It is an *accounting separation* of that trust property which becomes irrevocable when one of the husband-wife trustors dies. The accounting separation is necessary where certain untaxed assets pour over into the surviving trustor's estate. As a consequence, the first deceased trustor's subtrusts — even though irrevocable — are temporary only.

There are at least two subtrusts — often three — created when the first spousal trustor dies. These are:

X. Exempt Trust   }
                                 }   or other functionally
Y. Marital Deduction Trust   }   equivalent characterization
                                 }
Z. Residual Trust   }

The *Exempt Trust* sets aside the statutory exclusion amount that is not death taxed in the first decedent's gross estate. The amount of this exclusion is $1,000,000 (1 million) for death year 2003; $1,500,000 (1.5 million) for death years 2004 and 2005; and $2,000,000 (2 million) for death years 2006, 2007, and 2008. By setting aside the applicable exclusion amount into a separate subtrust of its own, it is not further death taxed when the surviving trustor dies. Because of no second death tax, the arrangement is often called a "Bypass Trust." The bypass amount is kept "on hold" until the commencement of distributions to beneficiaries after both trustors decease.

When a husband and wife set up a family (umbrella) trust, the first decedent spouse is allowed a **marital deduction** against that decedent's gross estate. This deduction can be any "qualified" amount so long as the unconsumed portion of it by the surviving trustor is included in that trustor's gross estate. No other person than the surviving spouse can withdraw money or property from this subtrust. This is why it is called the *Marital Deduction Trust*.

The *Residual Trust* consists of all "leftovers" after the amounts for subtrusts X and Y have been identified and set aside. And after all expenses, fees, debts, and taxes for the first decedent's estate have been paid. As a "residual" trust, it comprises after-tax money and property. This means that the assets in this subtrust can be distributed whenever, to whomever, and in whatever amounts, solely at the discretion of the surviving trustor/trustee. This subtrust takes on increasing significance when the gross estate of the first decedent trustor exceeds $3,000,000 or so.

To portray the sense of how these three subtrusts function, we present Figure 4.4. Different family trust instruments may use

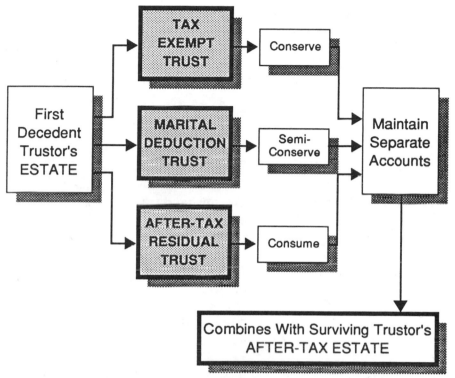

Fig. 4.4 - The Array of Subtrusts When First Trustor Dies

different terms from those we've listed above. This means that your trust preparer must go to great lengths to identify what shall be done—

AFTER DEATH OF FIRST TRUSTOR

. . . or caption words to this effect.

Death of Surviving Trustor

It is not until death of the surviving trustor that all property in the trust becomes irrevocable. After the survivor's estate is settled, the real distributive intent of the trust comes through. There are no longer any trustors to provide for. Thereupon, the trust assets "settle down" to become solely subject to the testamentary intent of the two creators of the trust. Both income and principal are distributed, depending on the discretionary powers of the successor trustee(s), and on the needs of each beneficiary.

Where do you find instructions for the distributions from the now irrevocable family trust?

Answer: Usually in a grouping of paragraphs under the heading of—

UPON DEATH OF SURVIVING TRUSTOR

. . . or words to this effect. The wording in these paragraphs coalesce both trustors' property into one overall **Trust Estate**. There is no longer an estate of the husband trustor to be settled, nor an estate of the wife trustor to be settled. There is just one trust estate to be administered, usually over many years.

The motivation behind most family trusts is to spread the distribution of money and property over a number of beneficiary years. The idea is to conserve the trust estate as much as possible so as to promote the greatest good to the greatest number of beneficiaries. This "good" is directed down generational lines: to children, grandchildren, and — in rare cases — great-grandchildren. When reaching the third generation down, many unknowns arise. Foremost is the problem of unborns and unnameds. There is also the problem of marriages, divorces, and remarriages. As a consequence, the trust estate becomes diluted finer and finer. All the while, the risks of controversy and litigation balloon. Rarely does any great-grandchild know of his or her great-grandparent. For these and other reasons, it is our view that the grandchildren of the trustors is about as far down as the trustors should go. Yes, we know that there are dynasties of wealth that recycle to the third, fourth, fifth, sixth, seventh, and et cetera generations. Wealth perpetuation is way beyond the scope of our discussion herein.

Successor Trustees & Powers

The husband and wife who create the family trust are its initial trustees. They are co-trustees even though only one may pay close attention to their property which is held in trust. Each continues to be a trustee until each dies, or until the survivor becomes incapacitated. At this point, one or more successor trustees need to be designated in the trust instrument.

In every family trust, there is a set of paragraphs often marked: SUCCESSOR TRUSTEE(S). The introductory wording to these paragraphs goes something like this—

> *If one of the Trustor-trustees cannot serve as a trustee, the other Trustor-trustee shall serve as the sole trustee. If both of the Trustor-trustees are unable to serve, then . . .*

The wording following the "then" is a succession of no more than three successively named trustees. Each of the three may be named as the First successor trustee, Second successor trustee, and Third successor trustee. Or, each may be named simply as "successor trustee" if the prior successor trustee is unable to serve.

For example, "If both of the Trustor-trustees are unable to serve as trustee, then"—

> *ROBERT R. JONES (son of Trustors) shall serve as Successor Trustee. If ROBERT is unable to serve as Successor Trustee, then SUSAN JONES SMITH (daughter of Trustors) shall serve as Successor Trustee. If SUSAN is unable to serve as Successor Trustee, then ROSS H. WHITE (nephew of Trustors) shall serve as Successor Trustee.*

We think it is generally **in**advisable to designate two successor trustees as co-trustees. Decisional competition and conflict too often can arise. This may lead to litigation to force removal of one of the co-trustees from office. Unnecessary litigation can deplete the trust estate prematurely.

The designation of three successor trustees should take care of most foreseeable family trust distributive intention. If not, a catchall successor clause can be embedded in the trust document. The catchall wording might read as—

> *If a vacancy should occur in the office of trustee, whether by reason of death, resignation, removal, or other cause, and no*

*successor trustee is appointed as provided in this instrument,
the Court shall appoint a new trustee to fill the vacancy.*

No matter who the successor trustee may be, he or she must be
given adequate authority to carry out the purpose of the trust. This
authority comprises all of those *powers now or hereafter conferred
on trustees by law.* In most instruments, these "statutory" powers
are itemized in detail (covering some three to five pages of trust
text). Additional powers are conferred with respect to discretionary
matters for the division or distribution of property in cash or in kind.
There are prohibited powers against using trust assets for a trustee's
own personal account or in any extravagant or speculative way on
behalf of the trust. A successor trustee can be removed from office
at any time for breach of duty or other cause.

Designation of Beneficiaries

When both spousal trustors are deceased, the successor trustee
must distribute the residual trust estate to one or more designated
beneficiaries. A "beneficiary" is the recipient of the estate of a
decedent. The term applies primarily to family members but may
include other designated persons. Trust property is conveyed to a
beneficiary with the expectation that it will be either consumed,
invested (for consumption later), or given away (to a more needy
person than the beneficiary). All such transfers are gratuitous —
meaning: *pure gifts.* There is no obligation for a beneficiary to
perform any services or pay any money to the trust or its trustee.
Once money or property is received by a designated beneficiary, the
beneficiary can do with it what he or she wants to. This is why
"living persons" are designated in the trust instrument.

Ideally, a family trust should consider making provision for five
classes of beneficiaries, as appropriate. These classes are:

I   — Interim beneficiaries
II   — Principal beneficiaries
III — Special needs beneficiaries
IV   — Issue of principal beneficiaries
V   — Trust termination beneficiary

The full names of all designated persons should be spelled out, followed by any nicknames or **a.k.a.**s (also known as). Always start with birth given names. A "full name" is the person's first name, middle name, and last name . . . all spelled out. In some cases, there may be two first names, or no middle name (use: **n.m.n.**), or two middle names, or two last names (sometimes hyphenated, depending on custom or country of origin). Spelling out names is essential for positive identity 5, 10, 15, or more years after the trust instrument is created. The spellings should either be in all cap lettering (e.g., DOUGLAS JAMES JONES) or bold lettering with initial caps (e.g., **Douglas James Jones**).

An *Interim beneficiary* (Class I above) is a person to whom a fixed sum of money (relatively small) or a specific property item (car, boat, piece of art, or jewelry) is bequeathed immediately after each trustor's death. Such bequests are one-time events. They are "interim" in that there is no expectation of any further distributions to said persons from the trust estate. This is one role of each trustor's pretrust will. This is also a way to limit the number of principal and other beneficiaries participating in the lion's share of the residual trust estate.

The *Principal beneficiaries* (Class II above) are the children and grandchildren of the deceased trustors, and possibly also the siblings (brothers and sisters) of the trustors. A *Special needs beneficiary* (Class III above) is a disabled, handicapped, spendthrift, or senile (advanced old age) person for whom the trustors have a moral or other obligation to provide for. Usually, a separate subtrust is established for each special needs person. The *Issue of principal beneficiaries* (Class IV above) are the children and children's children of the deceased principal beneficiaries.

The Class V *Trust termination beneficiary* — note the singular — is the "last person out" when the trust is finally terminated. Visit our Figure 4.5 to get a feel of what could emerge when having too many beneficiaries.

Should Limit the Number

Is there any limit to the number of beneficiaries that can participate in a family trust estate? Technically, the answer is "No."

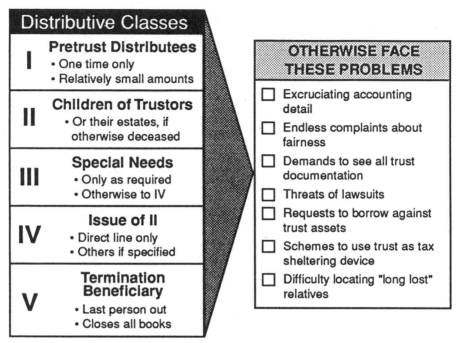

Fig. 4.5 - Blueprint for Limiting the Number of Trustors' Beneficiaries

There is no statutory limit. It could be any number from one to 100, presumably. There must be at least one beneficiary, if not a living person then some charitable organization (an exception to the "living person" definition, since a charitable organization will distribute to living persons).

One recent case has come to our attention where there were 25 — yes, 25 — living person beneficiaries. Since we actually computed the percentage participation of each, we list the results as follows:

4 persons received	1.8293% each or	7.3172%
4 " "	2.3333% each or	9.3334%
2 " "	3.0488% each or	6.0976%
5 " "	3.6585% each or	18.2925%
4 " "	4.6666% each or	18.6666%
2 " "	6.0000% each or	12.0000%
3 " "	6.0975% each or	18.2925%
1 person "	10.0000% or	10.0000%

25 Total beneficiaries   100.0000%
of residual estate

The amount of the residual estate distributable to all designated beneficiaries was slightly under $3 million ($2,878,542 to be more precise). It was thus necessary to compute each beneficiary's percentage to four decimal places. With so many beneficiaries with such precise individual percentages, the risk of distributive errors, and perceived errors, runs high. The logical question, therefore, is, "Isn't there some way to reduce this risk?"

Yes, there is. There are several ways. One way is to limit the number of principal beneficiaries and their issue (Classes II and IV in Figure 4.5) to between 5 and 10. Yes, this number is rather arbitrary; so, you pick a number. There just has to be some limit. The number of special needs beneficiaries (Class III) would rarely be more than one or two. The trust termination beneficiary (Class V) need only be one person. He or she could be a fiscally responsible person selected from Classes II or IV.

All other persons of favor by the trustors could be relegated to Class I (Interim beneficiaries). There could be any number of these persons. The way to limit the reduction of distributions to Classes II, III, and IV is to limit *each trustor's* Class I recipients to less than 10% of that trustor's net estate at time of his or her death. This way, the dominant portion of the two combined estates would be available for full trust administration.

Contingency Clauses Ad Nauseum

For each principal beneficiary named by the trustors, there is the possibility that that person may not survive the surviving trustor. Should this happen, one or more contingency clauses have to be inserted into the trust instrument. Unfortunately, one contingency clause leads to another, which leads to another . . . and so on.

Let us illustrate with the simplest case possible. The trustors have just one adult child whom we name *fictitiously*: **Janet J. Jones.** Janet is married and has three children, two of whom are married (with children). How would a trust preparer handle a contingency clause in this situation?

Answer: We'll cite from an actual trust instrument prepared by a reputable legal firm. The selected citation reads—

A. *Upon death of the Surviving Trustor, the trust estate shall be distributed to JANET J. JONES, if she survives the surviving trustor and if not, then to her issue then living as set forth in Section B hereinafter.*

B. *The share of a deceased child of the Trustors shall be divided into as many shares as the Trustors' deceased child left children surviving. Each share allocated to the living issue of a deceased child of the Trustors shall be retained and administered by the Trustee in a separate trust. The Trustee shall pay or apply for the benefit of the beneficiary so much net income and principal of the beneficiary's trust as the Trustee in the Trustee's sole discretion considers necessary for the beneficiary's proper health, support, maintenance, and education. The individual trusts hereunder shall be distributed outright and free of trust to their respective beneficiaries when the beneficiaries each attain the age of twenty-five. If any beneficiary does not survive until age twenty-five, his or her share shall be distributed to his or her estate.*

The above contingency clause is for just *one* adult child of the trustors. Can't you sense the clausal complexity when there are three children: two of whom are adults, married (with children), and one of whom is a minor (unmarried). What kind of contingency clause would address the minor child when he or she becomes an adult, gets married, has two children, gets divorced, gets remarried, and has two more children?

Now you know why some trust instruments can actually run 30 to 50 pages in length. The longer the span of time between the death of the first trustor and that of the surviving trustor, the more likely it is that family situations will change. A conscientious trust preparer must try to anticipate these changes while at the same time honoring the express wishes of the trustors.

Rule Against Perpetuities

All trust contracts are supposed to terminate at some point in time. Some specific date, event, or lapse of time after the death of some living individual is required to be prescribed. Unfortunately, many trust preparers tend to bury the termination requirement in fuzzy-worded clauses that a conscientious trustee cannot determine with certainty what the termination event is to be. The greater the value of the trust assets, and the longer the period of time between the deaths of the two creating trustors, the more likely the trust will continue ad infinitum.

Because family trusts involve the gratuitous transfers of money and property, there is temptation to treat the trust entity as a sheltering devise. The most common sheltering efforts involve tax avoidance, creditor protection, nonrepayment of loans, administrative expenditures, professional fees, and, yes, just plain old-fashioned grave robbing. These temptations increase markedly when a vacancy in trusteeship occurs and the Probate Court appoints a successor trustee. Court-appointed trustees tend to be attorneys, legal firms, and trust departments of financial institutions headed by attorneys. If the trust estate is significant enough, legally-trained trustees tend to perpetuate the sheltering aspects of a trust. We call this: *perpetuity milking*.

Because of the potential for perpetuity milking of trust assets, most states subscribe to the ***Uniform Statutory Rule Against Perpetuities***. California is one such state. Its Probate Code, Sections 21200 through 21231 — comprising about 1,280 words of text — sets forth two general anti-perpetuity rules. These two trust terminating rules are:

A. *The 21-year rule*: No later than 21 years after the death of a designated individual who was alive when the trust instrument was created.

B. *The 90-year rule*: The trust must terminate within 90 years of its creation.

One would think that the lead-in caption for terminating a trust would read: "When Trust is to be Terminated." No, the typical caption wording is—

Perpetuities Savings Clause

As a successor trustee, one has to know or be told that the word "perpetuities" is the court signal for describing the terminating event of a gratuitous trust. Family member successor trustees are not always aware of this covertness.

The most explicit example we could find is lifted from page 32 of a 37-page professionally prepared family trust. Under the covert caption above, the clause reads:

> *Unless sooner terminated in accordance with the provisions of this Agreement, all Trusts created under this Agreement shall be terminated twenty-one (21) years from and after the death of the last survivor of the Trustors and their issue living on the date of death of the first Trustor to die.*

Even this wording is fuzzy. Nevertheless, two events seem clear: (1) No termination until after the surviving trustor dies, and (2) There may be other provisions for terminating without waiting a full 21 years after the death of the last living beneficiary when the first trustor dies.

In the practical world, the living issue of the trustors (if adults and not mentally impaired) get together among themselves. They come to some agreement on the termination-of-trust activities well before the perpetuity time limits kick in.

5

WILLS & TRUSTS COMPARED

> The Similarities Are: (1) Same Soundness Of Mind Required, And (2) Same Inventory And Appraisement Immediately After Death. The DISSIMILARITIES Are: [1] Distribution Time Differences: 1 Year Or So For Wills; Up To 25 Years (Or So) For Trusts; [2] Dollar Magnitude Of Distributions: $1 Million Or So For Wills; Multi-Million For Trusts; [3] Wills Are Simple; Trusts Are Complex; [4] Only Certain Wills Avoid Probate; Most Trusts Do So; [5] Most Wills Avoid Death Tax Whereas Trusts Over $3 Million Can Not; [6] For Property Transactions, Wills Require "Letters Testamentary" vs. A "Certification Document" For Trusts.

We are comparing Wills and Trusts because each has advantages and disadvantages that the other does not have. For example, one can go through life without ever creating a trust. But no responsible person should go through life without a will. Which brings us once again to our premise: *Everyone needs a will; not everyone needs a trust.* Even when creating a trust, it is preceded by a will. A pretrust will is quite perfunctory when it dumps "most everything" into a trust.

There are two key characterizing differences between wills and trusts. These are: (1) age of the maker(s) and (2) extent of assets (or degree of wealth) involved. It is quite unlikely that 30-year-old newly marrieds with one infant child would have any true need for a trust. Especially when the trust must terminate 21 years after the infant, as an adult, dies leaving one or more infants of his or her own. There are far too many human contingencies to be perceived.

Nor is it likely that the newly married couple above would have sufficient wealth to justify the cost and complexity of preparing a family trust. More likely, instead, are persons approaching or in their retirement years — 60 to 80 years of age or so. Many retirement-age persons may need a trust, regardless of wealth. Obviously, with several adult children, some of whom may have children of their own, the greater the retiree wealth, the greater the need for a gratuitous trust. The level of wealth (at any age) is certainly a major factor, but so, too, is maturational age.

Consequently, in this chapter, we want to place the two testamentary documents side by side and compare their similarities and differences. It's not a matter of which is better for all circumstances. It's a matter of which is better at which point in time, and which can be changed more easily, when circumstances change. Let us start with the similarities with respect to testamentary capacity.

Identical Soundness of Mind

Whether preparing a will document or a trust document, the maker thereof must be of sound mind. The focal emphasis is on soundness of *mind* regardless of one's physical well being, medical condition, or marital status. So long as the document maker knows who he/she is; knows what he/she is doing; knows the extent of his/her property holdings; knows the living persons to whom he/she intends to transfer the property; and knows the person(s) or successor persons(s) whom he/she has appointed as Executor (of a will) and Trustee (of a trust), the document maker exhibits true soundness of mind.

Soundness of mind is fundamentally a legal requirement. But it is also a financial and taxation requirement. A "sound mind" does not require that a document maker be both a financial genius and a tax expert. All such maker need do is to have the presence of mind to engage knowledgeable professionals when needed. Our position is that "knowledgeable professionals" should be sought *before* seeking an attorney. Attorneys are not the best conveyers of helpful knowledge. They tend to be intimidating and "scare off" knowledge-seeking inquirers.

One indicator of lacking complete soundness of mind is turning everything over to an attorney before seeking information elsewhere. Turning "everything over" to an attorney is the scared-off lazy person's approach to purely personal and family matters. Other persons, either through their own experiences with wills and trusts, or through their own research and readings on the subject, can offer a pointer or two that some attorney could miss altogether. Although attorneys can be good persons, they should not be your sole source of information for testamentary decision making.

Soundness of mind is also a function of age. A young couple in their late 20s or early 30s simply don't know what they don't know. Knowledge and wisdom are acquired incrementally with increasing age. This means that their chosen testamentary document must change throughout their lifespan and lifestyle.

On the other hand, an elderly couple in their 70s or 80s may find that their soundness of minds starts to diminish. Senility and aches and pains with attendant medications creep in to impair their judgments. Elderly persons are most vulnerable to undue influence by their children, by their siblings, and by their peers. This often leads to confusion. The result is that: everything is turned over to an attorney. Talk about "undue influence," this is it. Many attorneys eye the distributive wealth of retirees with covetous intentions in mind. Hence, this is the time for adult children to take a more protective role in their parents' estate plans.

Estate Accounting the Same

Whether one has a will, a trust, or a combination of the two, when a person dies, an *estate* is created. This is solely by "operation of law." All assets of the decedent are frozen in place, temporarily. This is to allow adequate time — 9 to 15 months, typically — for accounting and taxation purposes. During the same hold-up time, probate may or may not be required. This is where wills and trusts differ. But as to accounting and taxation matters, it makes no difference whether a testator (will maker) or trustor (trust creator) is the decedent.

When a testator or trustor dies, what are the accounting and taxation matters that have to be resolved?

Answer: They are many. So, we'll touch only on the highlights. They all have one central theme in common, namely: **Inventory and Appraisement** of all assets of the decedent. Three major sequential steps are required:

One — Establish the *gross estate* of the decedent;

Two — Claim the *allowable deductions* against the decedent's gross estate; and

Three — Compute and pay, or recompute as necessary, all taxes associated with the decedent's death: past, present, and future.

A decedent's gross estate consists of one or more of the following classifications of property:

A — Real Estate
B — Stocks & Bonds
C — Mortgages, Notes, & Cash
D — Insurance on Decedent's Life
E — Jointly Owned Property
F — Other Miscellaneous Property
G — Gifts During Decedent's Life
H — Powers of Appointment
I — Annuities

A "power of appointment" is the right of a decedent (when alive) to enjoy all or part of the property of someone else which is in trust, under contract, or sequestered by insurance or other arrangement. An "annuity" is a contract for payments over a period of time referenced to the annuitant's life expectancy (who is now deceased). Any power or annuity exercisable in favor of the decedent **is included** in his/her estate.

When the above inventory is done and all property items are fair market valued, the decedent's *gross estate* is established. From this gross estate, certain deductions are allowed. The most common of said deductions are—

1. Funeral expenses
2. Administrative expenses & professional fees
3. Debts of the decedent
4. Mortgages & liens against decedent's property
5. Casualty & theft losses to the gross estate
6. Bequests to surviving spouse, if any
7. Charitable bequests & similar gifts, if any
8. Family-owned business deduction
9. Qualified conservation easement deduction

When these deductibles are totaled and subtracted from the gross estate, a *net estate* is establish. [Gross minus deductions allowed equals "net."]

There is a statutory exclusion against all net estates before any death tax applies. Suffice it to say that the exclusion (tax exempt portion) ranges between $1,000,000 (1 million) and $3,500,000, depending on year of death. Even if there is no federal death tax imposed, there may be state inheritance taxes, certain foreign taxes, prior-to-death income taxes, estate income taxes, property taxes, sales taxes, employer taxes (for the decedent's business, if any), and other taxes that, uncannily, jump out of the woodwork when an estate is being settled.

After subtracting all taxes due and payable by the estate, a *distributable estate* emerges. It is this distributable estate — **not** the gross estate — that is subject to distribution by will or by trust. Until such amount is unequivocally established, it makes no difference whether the decedent is a testator or trustor. We summarize these points and show their relationship in Figure 5.1.

Distribution Time Difference

Once the distributable estate of a decedent is known, the distribution process differs markedly between wills and trusts.

In the case of a will, the distribution process is a one event, one time affair. Except for a small contingency for last-minute unforeseens, the distributions exhaust the entire will estate. There is nothing left for subsequent distributions. There's no follow-on

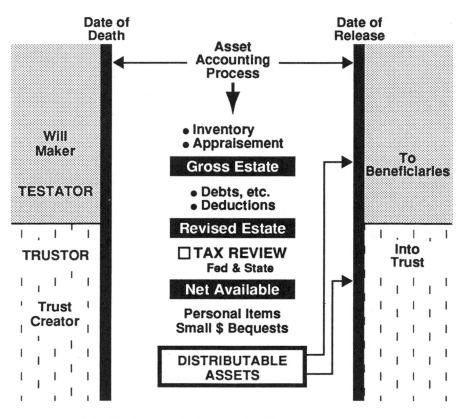

Fig. 5.1 - The Immediate Accounting Process After Any Death

except for finalized accounting for closing the books on the decedent's property. Let us illustrate.

Suppose that a distributable estate is $1,364,890. This is after all debts, expenses, and taxes have been paid. There would be some further relatively small diminution of this amount for will closing costs: professional fees, executor fees, administrative expenses, and incidental last-minute claims. Suppose that 2.56% (or $34,890) were set aside for closing cost purposes. This would leave $1,330,000 (1 million, 330 thousand dollars) for distribution to those beneficiaries expressly named in the will document. Thus, over $1.3 million would be distributed gratuitously (free of tax) all at one time. The span of time involved would probably run between 9 and 15 months after the testator's death.

Had the same distributable amount of $1,364,890 been assigned to a trust, there would be no immediate closing-cost set-asides. Generally speaking, the trust instrument would require that the same total money be converted into income-producing property. Examples would be dividend-paying stock, interest-paying bonds, and rental-income-paying real estate. Thus, the trust estate would consist of two components: income and principal. The idea would be to preserve and manage the property until other provisions of the trust agreement materialized.

At some time later, distributions of principal would be made. This might be anywhere from a few years after the trustor's death to as many as 25 to 30 years. Even then, instead of a one-time distribution to all beneficiaries, there more likely would be multiple mini-distributions over multiple years. Any distributions of *principal* to the beneficiaries would be free of tax to them.

In the meantime, the trust is generating income and, possibly, capital gains. The income and capital gains are distributed annually to the beneficiaries. Since these are **income** distributions (not distributions of principle), they are taxable to the beneficiaries. The overall net effect is that, distribution wise, a trust is more time enduring than is a will.

Dollar Value Distinctions?

There's one question that often comes up re the choice between a will and a trust. Does the dollar value of a person's distributable assets make a difference whether he/she chooses a will or a trust?

The careful answer is: Not really. There is no statutory guidance on this, whatsoever. One could distribute $5,000,000 (five million) or much more from a will estate . . . and be done with it. There's no prohibition against doing so.

Yes, one could make a large-dollar-amount distribution from his/her will estate, but would it be prudent to do so? Wouldn't the spread-out of distributions from a trust be better? Wouldn't the spread out over extended time be more indicative of a sound mind than a one-time dumping of $5,000,000?

Observational experience reveals that when a beneficiary receives a large sum of money — whether from a will or from a trust — that money is spent almost immediately. "It's free money," the recipient's reasoning goes, "so why not spend it freely?" Instead of using the money to get completely out of debt, and put some away for a rainy day, it is spent on luxury items (cars, boats, aircraft), fancy clothes, extended vacations, gambling, and/or investing heavily in speculative stock schemes. We know one such case when the wife inherited $900,000 (rounded) from her deceased father. She and her husband immediately took off and visited a gambling casino In just three days, the entire $900,000 was gone! How foolish with money can some beneficiaries get?

Most testators and trustors work an entire lifetime to build an adequate nest egg for major medical needs, retirement savings, and nursing home care. Their only expectation is that their heirs apparent be mindful and prudent with the windfall of money being left to said heirs. Ordinary reasoning suggests, therefore, that the greater the amount of money being distributed, the more beneficial a trust arrangement would be.

"Where's the line of demarcation?" you ask. "When is a will more beneficial than a trust, and vice versa?" Since you asked, we must respond.

In our opinion, *one million dollars* ($1,000,000) is a good distinguishing line.

If a distributable estate amounted to $1 million or less and there was more than one adult beneficiary, a will would serve a decedent's testamentary intent admirably. For example, suppose there were three qualified heirs to a $1 million will estate. If they shared equally in said estate, each would receive a lump-sum distribution of $333,333. Without any spendthrift apologizing, each recipient could pay off his/her home mortgage, pay off all credit cards, put some money away for children's education, and take a modest but well deserved family vacation. Even if there were only two equal-sharing heirs, the money would be spent wisely and, we believe, with the posthumous approval of the decedent.

On the other hand, as an estate's distributable value exceeds $1 million and advances into the multi-million dollar range, trusts make more economic sense. There are three reasons for this. One, appropriate spendthrift clauses can be incorporated to limit any single lump-sum distribution to a specified maximum amount.

Two, one or more subtrusts can be established to fund for life a surviving spouse, physically/mentally handicapped person, and elderly parents requiring nursing home and twilight care. And, three, a grand distribution clause can require that the bulk of the distributions be made over a term-certain number of years for each "regular" beneficiary.

Wills are Simply Simpler

From the drift of earlier comments in this chapter and others preceding, one message should be coming through. That message is: Wills are fundamentally simpler than are trusts. Several factors account for the simplicity of wills relative to trusts. The principal fact is *administrative time* after a decedent's death. The term "administrative time" begins at date of death and ends when all distributable assets are distributed. In the case of an ordinary will, the span of administrative time is from about nine months to, in rare cases, 15 months. In this period of time, the decedent's assets have to be inventoried and valued, the beneficiaries have to be identified, and all debts, expenses, and fees associated with the decedent have to be paid. Once this is done, the administrator (called: *Executor*) disburses the residual money . . . and that's it. There is no long-term management of the money as in the case of a trust.

In contrast, a trust administrator (called: *Trustee*) has to preserve and manage a decedent's money over relatively long periods of time. How long? At least more than one year to as many, perhaps, as 25 years or longer. During this greater administrative time, more things can happen. More things can go wrong; more beneficiaries emerge (due to births, deaths, divorces, remarriages): and more judgmental conflicts between trustees, trust professionals, and expectant beneficiaries. And to top this all off, the more money involved — $1 million, $5 million, $10 million, etc. — the more safeguards that have to be imposed. It is only natural, therefore, that trusts are simply more complex than wills. We try to summarize this simplicity-versus-complexity aspect for you in Figure 5.2.

All of this leads to one realistic conclusion. That is, a will lends itself to self-preparation, whereas a trust does not. This is a

Comparative Items		WILLS	TRUSTS
1)	No. of Pages	3 to 5 pages Few contingencies	30 to 50 pages Many contingencies
2)	Administration Time	6 to 15 *Months*	1 to 25 *Years* (or so)
3)	Joint Spousal Document	**No**: Separate will for each spouse	**Yes**: Adds complexity; separate provisions for each spousal death
4)	Title of Administrator	Executor A family member	Trustee Provision for court appointee
5)	Likely Problems	• Simultaneous deaths • Some disinherited kin	• Takeover by covetous attorneys • Distributions minimized
6)	Property Trans-actional Authority	Letters Testamentary	Certification Document
7)	No. of Distributees	Tends to be fewer due to shorter administration time	Increases the longer the surviving trustor lives
8)	Primary Function	Liquify & distribute assets promptly	Conserve assets and invest for income
9)	Probate Required	**No**: For "small estates" **Yes**: For all others	**No**: In general **Yes**: When disputes arise

Fig. 5.2 - Abbreviated Analysis of Why Wills are Simpler Than Trusts

fortunate aspect. There are simply more non-millionaires in the U.S. than there are millionaires. And, by extension, there are more millionaires than billionaires. This means that "ordinary people" — with a few pointers gleaned from sample professionally-prepared wills — can write their own wills. And they can change them frequently as their beneficiaries change and as their distributable assets grow towards the one million dollar ($1,000,000) mark.

Estates Under $100,000

We want to let you in on a little secret that attorneys seldom tell you about. It is called the: *Affidavit Procedure* for small estates. This is a nonprobate procedure which applies irrespective of whether a will or a trust is involved. The procedure is set forth in the Probate Code of the state in which the decedent was domiciled. Different states, different threshold amounts. In California, for example, the nonprobate threshold is $100,000. There are also certain exclusions from this amount. Let us explain.

Section 13100 of the California Probate Code [CPC] is fully titled: *Estates under $100,000; Authorization to act without procuring letters of administration or awaiting probate*. The term "Letters of Administration," is like a general power of attorney established by a probate court after a decedent's demise. Said document confirms the administrator's legal powers and duties with respect to the decedent's property. Also called: "Letters Testamentary," said document constitutes the initial phase of probate proceedings. The affidavit procedure bypasses the probate process for small estates. This, we think, illustrates legislative wisdom in the real world.

The thrust of CPC § 13100 reads primarily as—

Excluding the property described in Section 13050, if the gross value of the decedent's real and personal property in this state [California] *does not exceed one hundred thousand dollars ($100,000) and if 40 days have elapsed since the death of the decedent, the successor of the decedent may, without procuring letters of administration or awaiting probate of the will, do any of the following with respect to the* [decedent's] *property.*

The excluded items under CPC § 13050 are: (1) joint-tenancy property, (2) multi-party accounts, (3) registered vehicles, and (4) compensatory amounts due the decedent. We'll tell you more about the affidavit process in Chapter 11: The Probative Process. Meanwhile, Figure 5.3 depicts the very point that we are getting at.

Said point is that, while living trusts are well known for their ability to avoid probate, wills can be structured in a way that they,

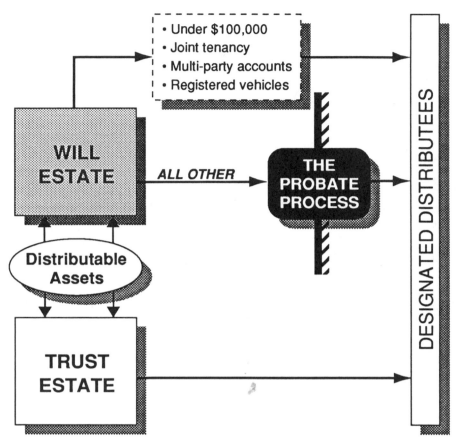

Fig. 5.3 - The Nonprobate Aspects of a Will Estate vs. a Trust Estate

too, can avoid probate. The smaller the gross value of an estate, the easier it is to avoid probate. However, probate avoidance with a will becomes less and less feasible when said estate approaches or exceeds $1 million ($1,000,000).

Best Argument for a Trust

Administratively and legally, there is no lower limit to the value of a decedent's estate that can be assigned to a trust. The best lower limit answer that we can find is CPC § 15408: ***Trust with uneconomically low principal***. The essence of this section is that—

If the trust principal does not exceed twenty thousand dollars ($20,000) in value, the trustee has the power to terminate the trust.

Thus, $20,000 is clearly the lower limit for creating a trust. Is there any upper limit?

No. There appears to be no upper limit whatsoever. A trustor's assets could be one million, 10 million, 100 million, 1,000 million (1 billion) . . . or whatever. Yet, from our perspective, there's a practical limit for those who would read this book and derive benefit from it. So, we pick a number. Our pick is between 10 and 30 million dollars: 20 million on average. This number represents about 10 times a decedent's estate-tax-exclusion amount of $2,000,000 (for death years 2006, 2007, and 2008).

Persons with distributive assets greater than $20,000,000 would seek advice only from prestigious law firms. Said firms, more than likely, would devise various interlocking trusts whose objectives would be wealth secretion (probably in offshore trusts), charitable (private) foundations, and tax avoidance schemes. These matters are simply beyond our expertise and scope of discussion.

Nevertheless, on the assumption that a family trust arrangement is purely a gratuitous disposition of assets over an extended period of time, a trust serves a purpose which no will alone could possibly do. A trust **can avoid** probate. As pointed out previously in Chapter 4, the key to doing so is having the bulk of a trustor's property in the name of the trust, before either trustor dies. Regardless of all else that can be said comparing wills and trusts, probate avoidance is the very best argument that can be made for a trust. Within reason, this argument alone surmounts all of the complexity and disadvantages of a 30- to 50-page trust instrument.

There's just one precaution: probate avoidance and *tax* avoidance are NOT the same. For a $20 million taxable estate, for example, $2 million would be tax exempt. Thereupon, $18 million would be transfer taxed at around $9 million (as of December, 2004). Other than giving the entire $18 million to charity, there is no legal way to avoid the estate tax: trust or no trust. In year 2009, the exemption amount is scheduled to jump to $3.5 million with a tax rate on the excess above this amount at 45%.

Certification of Trust

When both trustors are deceased or incapacitated, the first designated successor trustee becomes the asset manager for the (now irrevocable) multi-million-dollar trust. When word to this effect gets around, strained business dealings erupt. Every transactional order to buy, sell, or exchange an asset is countered with a demand. The demand is to produce the original trust instrument (its full 30 to 50 pages) and point out the exact paragraph, section, and sentence that authorizes the instructed transaction. If there is no exact "point out," a court order is required. This is called: *trustee taunting*. Much of this taunting is backed by covetous attorneys whose objective is to cause the trustee to falter, make mistakes, and provide cause for removal. The court-replaced trustee then becomes an attorney, legal firm, or trust company (headed by an attorney).

Enter now the role of a document called: *Certification of Trust*. This is a 3- to 5-page condensation of the trust instrument with predominant emphasis on the legal powers of a successor trustee. The successor trustees are identified, as is the trust property. The state law authorization for accepting the certification as a legal document is cited. In California, said authorization is CPC § 18100.5: *Certification of trust; contents; trust document excerpt copies; certification reliance; liability*.

The idea is that a Certificate of Trust document has the same legal force and power of a court order. To confirm the effect, the document must be officially recorded in county records. Once the recording is done, a copy of the certification may be presented to, and retained by, any person demanding adequate legal authority before carrying out a property transaction. The idea also is to free the property transactor from any liability for any errors that might arise, when carrying out the instructions of the successor trustee.

Representative wording in the closing paragraph of the certification may read (in most part) as—

Reliance on This Certification. This certification is made in accordance with Section _____ of the _____ Probate Code, a copy of which is attached hereto. Any transaction entered into by a person acting in reliance on this certification shall be enforceable against the trust assets. Any person who refuses to accept this certification . . . will be liable for damages . . . incurred as a result of that refusal.

In other words, where active property management is anticipated, a supplement to the basic trust instrument is required. Otherwise, endless legal costs can deplete prematurely the trust assets. A certification document adds a bit of complexity to a trust, when compared with the simplicity of a will.

Organizational Formalities

Trust contracts truly can become quite complex. For most family arrangements, contingency clauses, if read in their entirety, can be overwhelming. Professional trust preparers try to ease access to the pertinent information therein by organizing their work product with clear captions of meaning. As a general pattern, all start with a series of headliners sequenced as: ARTICLE I, ARTICLE II, ARTICLE III, etc., each with a suitable caption of its own. Each Article then is followed by numbered Sections 1.01, 2.01, 3.01, etc., each section having a suitable caption of its own.

Let us illustrate with a relatively simple trust. Here we go—

ARTICLE I: CREATION OF TRUST

ARTICLE II: TRUST ESTATE

ARTICLE III: RIGHTS & POWERS OF TRUSTORS

ARTICLE IV: WHILE BOTH TRUSTORS ALIVE

ARTICLE V: AFTER DEATH OF TRUSTOR(S)

ARTICLE VI: SUCCESSOR TRUSTEES

ARTICLE VII: CONCLUDING PROVISIONS

ARTICLE VIII: EXECUTION & FUNDING

More complicated trust contracts often have an **ARTICLE XII** titled as: MISCELLANEOUS PROVISIONS.   Said ARTICLE XII may be sectioned as follows—

12.01 — *Jurisdiction; No Court Supervision*

12.02 — *Perpetuities Savings Clause*

12.03 — *Discretionary Distributions*

12.04 — *Trustee's Reliance on Beneficiary's Statements*

12.05 — *Trustee's Discretion re a Minor*

12.06 — *Trustee's Discretion on Invasion of Principal*

12.07 — *Distributions in Good Faith*

12.08 — *No Outright Distribution to an Incompetent*

12.09 — *Additions to Trust*

12.10 — *No-Contest Clause*

12.11 — *Spendthrift Clause*

12.12 — *Definition of Certain Terms*

Compared with the above, wills are organized into separate (rather short) paragraphs with no caption.   The paragraphs are numbered simply as: FIRST, SECOND, THIRD, . . . TWELFTH.   Digesting the impact of a 3-to-5 page document (such as a will) does not require the same focal discipline of a 30-to-50-page instrument (such as a trust).

6

EXECUTOR, TRUSTEE ROLES

An Executor Is Appointed By The Maker Of A Will; A Trustee Is Appointed By The Creator Of A Trust. The Roles And Duties Of Each Appointee Differ Substantially. Whereas An Executor Focuses On Inventory, Appraisement, And Distribution Of Property Within A Short Period Of Time, A Trustee Seeks To Invest, Manage, And "Grow" The Property Over An Extended Period Of Time. Should A Trustee Not Produce The Results Sought, He Is Criticized And Threatened With Lawsuits By Disgruntled Beneficiaries. His Best Defense Is A Showing Of Due Diligence And Care In Annual "Reports Of Account."

Neither a Will nor a Trust can be activated until after each maker thereof dies. By "activating," we mean carrying out the express instructions within each testamentary document. Who carries out these instructions? Is it some attorney who is called in the day after the document maker dies?

Answer: No! The activator is *not* an attorney. Nor should it be. The activator of a will is the **Executor** thereof; the activator of a trust is the **Trustee** thereof. The executor, and, separately, the trustee are the personal appointees of each document maker. Most often, it is the surviving spouse who is the first appointee. This is followed by the appointment of an adult child with a proven sense of responsibility and respect for the deceased parent. In many cases, the same spouse or same child is appointed as both an Executor

and Trustee. When this occurs, confusion arises. Even without "dual-status" appointments, confusion arises.

Confusion arises because there is not a clear understanding of the operational role of an executor, as contrasted with that of a trustee. The two roles are distinct and separate from each other. An executor is a person who takes charge of a will estate to accomplish many things in a relatively short period of time. A trustee, on the other hand, is a person who manages money and oversees the financial affairs of the trust estate over an extended period of time.

There is one basic factual difference between executor and trustee roles. The roles are SEQUENTIAL to each other: NOT concurrent. The executor role has to be completed first. If there is no tie-in with a trust, there is no trustee role to be performed. Where there is an active and ongoing trust, the trustee takes over from the executor.

Accordingly, in this chapter, we try our best to present a working understanding of the role differences between executors and trustees. Once death occurs, the first appointee on the property scene is the executor. Many accounting and taxation tasks — some rather complicated — have to be performed. This is why it is important that the executor be "left alone" (so to speak) to complete his tasks fully. Except in those situations where purely legal issues arise (such as the need for probate, interpretations of a document, or real property retitlings), legal counseling is not a prerequisite for the roles of executor or trustee. Common sense and devotion to duty are far more essential.

Appointment Process: Executor

An executor is nominated and appointed by the testator of a will. The customary practice is to first appoint one's spouse (if any) and then appoint one or more adult children (if any). If there are no adult children or, if adults but not capable of serving in an executor role, then one or more siblings of the testator or one or more nephews or nieces is so appointed. The testator has complete freedom to appoint whomever he wants. Each appointee, however, should have reasonable capability in handling business affairs, and be prudent with respect to the property of the testator.

A testator's appointment wording in his will could go something like this—

I hereby nominate and appoint my spouse, ___(full name)___ as Executor and direct that __(he/she)__ shall be empowered to act on my behalf without bond. Should, for any reason, my spouse be unable to act or continue as my Executor, then I nominate and appoint __(my adult child or other)__ , ____(full name)____ as Executor to likewise act without bond. . . . Etc.

Usually, a surviving spouse and **two** successor executors are named. Due to the relatively short period of executor service time (9 to 15 months or so), rarely is there a need for naming more than two successor executors. The presumption is that the person appointed as a successor executor is well known to, and personally trusted by, the testator. The bit about power to act "without bond" means that no posting of security money by the executor is required.

Because a joint will by husband and wife is not legally condoned, two "mirror" wills are often written at the same time. Often, but not always, each mirror will appoints the same two successor executors. Such is usually not the case where there has been a remarriage and different adult children, siblings, and nephews/nieces are involved.

Appointment Process: Trustee

In the case of a trust, the appointment process is quite different from that of appointing executors in two separate will documents. The difference arises from the fact that a family trust instrument is a joint document between husband and wife. There is also the fact that a longer trustee serving time is (or may be) involved: from one or two years to many years. Anticipating the longer time, provision needs to be made for a succession of appointed trustees.

In a family trust, the husband and wife serve as trustor-trustees until both spouses die. When this happens, a section titled: *Successor Trustees* is set forth in the trust document. Said provision usually is found past midway through the numerous pages of the instrument.

The successor trustee appointment wording may go something like this—

> *If both the Trustor-trustees are unable to serve as trustee, then __(name #1)__ shall serve as Successor Trustee. If __(name #1__ is unable to serve as Successor Trustee, then __(name #2)__ shall serve as Successor Trustee. If __(name #2)__ is unable to serve . . ., then __(name $3)__ shall serve. . . . If, for whatever reason, a vacancy should occur in the office of trustee and no other successor trustee is appointed as provided herein, the Court shall appoint a new trustee to fill the vacancy.*

The term "Court" refers to the Probate Court having jurisdiction at the time the trust instrument was created. Usually, the official name and location of the court is clearly stated in the trust document itself.

Our position is that court-appointed trustees should be avoided if at all possible. Said appointees tend to be attorneys, law firms, or the trust departments of financial institutions (headed by attorneys). Dragging out the trust operation unnecessarily, fee milking, and professional aloofness become the order of the day.

A preferable alternative would be to empower the last serving trustee to appoint a successor trustee within the family structure. Said appointment would be based on consultation with all beneficiaries, and on the written consent of the majority of them. Then, only then, if no consensus can be reached, seek a court appointee. When doing so, go to the extra effort of requesting the court to consider a nominated close business friend of the family to be its appointee.

In a trust arrangement lasting multiple years, it is preferable to state only the successor trustee's full name. There is no need to identify at that time who the particular appointee is. Said identity will become known in due time, when that trustee actually accepts the duties imposed upon him or her. Otherwise, too much family bickering and jostling over property assets could evolve. This could lead to one or more appointees prematurely renouncing their trusteeship roles. Frequent vacancies and litigative pursuits re said vacancies promote exactly the "right brew" that the legal profession loves for continuing its involvement in trust affairs.

Duties & Powers of Executor

When the maker of a will dies — whether an ordinary will or a pretrust will — the appointed executor "takes charge." There are many, many things to do. None of the tasks, however, needs to start until well after the obituary notices have been published, and the funeral and/or memorial services have been concluded. At some point as these matters are taking place, the executor may be asked: "How many copies of the **death certificate** do you want?"

Without any hesitation, answer "Ten." While an executor may not need exactly 10 copies, he will need close to this number. There is always someone or some entity or property holder wanting "proof" of death. Common practice these days recognizes that the holder of the death certificates for the decedent is the executor of the decedent's estate. Said person is also called the *personal representative* of the decedent.

The duties and powers of the personal representative of a decedent's estate are set forth in the probate code for the state where the decedent resided at time of death. In the case of California, for example, **CPC § 9650** reads in part as—

(1)   The personal representative has the right to and shall take possession or control of, all of the property of the decedent to be administered in the decedent's estate, and shall collect all debts due to the decedent or to the estate.

(2)   The personal representative is entitled to receive the rents, issues, and profits from the real and personal property in the estate until the estate is distributed.

(3)   The personal representative shall pay taxes on, and take all steps reasonably necessary for the management, protection, and preservation of, the estate in his or her possession.

Everything belonging to the decedent — his assets *and* liabilities — must pass through the executor's hands The only satisfactory accounting way to do this is to establish an estate checking account for the decedent. As we depict in Figure 6.1, an executor is the focus hub for all property accounting activities.

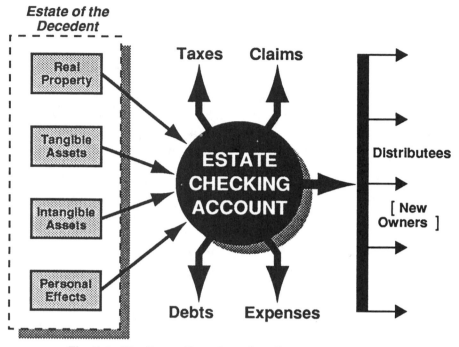

Fig. 6.1 - The Focus Function of an Executor: In and Out

Role of "Letters Testamentary"

So much for the statutory duties and powers of an executor (personal representative). He/she . . . "shall take possession and control" . . . of the decedent's property. What happens if some recalcitrant holder of property (real estate, stock, mutual fund, business interest, insurance policy, bank account) flat out refuses to honor the executor's request to take possession and control!

First off, you know that the refuser has had prior legal coaching on the matter. The refuser wants the person who claims to be the executor to prove who he is, and to produce *Letters Testamentary* confirming his authority "to take possession," etc. To get these "letters," the executor has to file the original will with the clerk of the probate court. Then he has to file a petition and public notice of the decedent's death.

The above steps constitute the "commencement" of probate proceedings. It is not always necessary to complete the process, but getting letters is essential. Otherwise, the executor can be subjected to much taunting and baiting by those who want to gain from the "free use" of a decedent's money and property. The procedure for getting legal letters is quite simple. There are preprinted check-the-box forms for doing so. In Figure 6.2 we present an abridgment of the California petition-for-letters form. Ask the probate clerk's office where you may buy these and other related forms commercially. If you get no response from the probate clerk, visit the county law library nearby and make similar inquiry.

To impress you with the true need for Letters Testamentary, we cite CPC § 8001. This California probate code section is fully titled: *Executor named in will; time to petition before right to be personal representative is waived.* This section reads in full as—

Unless good cause for delay is shown, if a person named in a will as executor fails to petition the court for administration of the estate within 30 days after the person has knowledge of the death of the decedent and that the person is named as executor, the person may be held to have waived the right to appointment as personal representative.

The idea here is to test the statutory awareness of an executor to his right — and duty — to petition for letters testamentary. If he does not do so "within 30 days," some covetous attorney appears on the scene to take charge. Do note, however, that "good cause for delay" can be shown.

There are three valid causes for delay in petitioning for letters testamentary. Foremost is that the bulk of the decedent's estate is in joint tenancy, community property, or other multiple-ownership form. Except for a recalcitrant property holder, full bore probate is not required. A second good cause would be that the will itself states that the executor shall exercise his authority under the rules of Independent Administration. (See the third checkbox in Figure 6.2.) A third good cause is that the bulk of the decedent's property is in

Name & Address of Petitioner	For Court Use
Name & Address of Superior Court	
Name of Decedent	
PETITION FOR	Case No. _____
	Hearing Date _____
☐ Probate of Will ☐ _____	Dept. _____
☐ Letters Testamentary ☐ _____	Time _____
☐ Independent Administration	

1. Petitioner requests that:
   a. ☐ Decedent's Will be admitted to probate
   b. ☐ He be appointed Executor with Letters Testamentary.
   c. ☐ Authority be granted to administer estate independently.
   d. ☐ Bond not be required.
2. Decedent died on:
   a. ☐ A resident of the county of _____
   b. ☐ A nonresident with estate in the county of _____
   c. ☐ Character and estimated value of the estate:
      ☐ Real property $_____
      ☐ Personal property $_____
   d. ☐ Will waves bond.
   e. ☐ Copy of decedent's Will dated _____   is attached.
   f. ☐ Proposed Executor is named in Will.
   g. ☐ Proposed Executor is resident of
3. Decedent is survived by _____
4. Decedent's will does ☐ does not ☐ preclude independent administration.
5. Names, residences, relationships, and ages of heirs, devisees, and legatees named in Will are attached.
6. Petitioner requests publication in _____

Dated: _____   _____/s/_____

  I declare under penalty of perjury that the foregoing is true and correct and is executed on _____   at_____

_____   _____/s/_____
(Typed or printed name)   (Signature of petitioner)

Fig. 6.2 - Abridged Format of Petition for Letters Testamentary

the name of his/her trust, and that no Certificate of Trust document is available.

The court hearing for authenticating the petition for letters is quite perfunctory. Unless some adversary of the executor is present who objects, the matter is a routine calendar call by the clerk. The presiding judge asks: "Any objections?" If no response, the judge scribbles his/her signature on the certification document and hands it to the clerk. The clerk stamps the court's official seal on the Letters Testamentary document, then gives a copy to the petitioning executor. The judge states: "Next case." Then moves on.

IRS Form 706; Yes or No?

From a property-possession-and-control point of view, there is one single-most important accounting task for an executor. It is the inventory and appraisement of the decedent's property, and the computation of his gross estate. The best guideline sequence for doing this is IRS Form 706. This tax form is officially titled: *U.S. Estate (and Generation-Skipping Transfer) Tax Return*. This is otherwise known as a *transfer tax* return. Form 706 is a *very* formidable tax document. Its objective is to impose tax on the privilege of transferring property gratuitously to others, who themselves pay no tax on said property. The threshold for the 706 tax is fairly high: $1,500,000 (1.5 million) for death years 2004 and 2005; $2,000,000 (2 million) for years 2006 through 2008; and $3,500,000 (3.5 million) for 2009 and thereafter.

As is self-evident from these threshold amounts, not every executor will be required to file Form 706. Nevertheless, we urge every executor to use the 40-or-so-page form as a checklist-type outline for resurrecting all assets and all liabilities of the decedent. It is a truly remarkable checklist for "missing nothing" with respect to a full accounting of a decedent's estate. We'll discuss Form 706 in more detail in Chapter 11: The Taxation Process.

If no Form 706 is officially required, it is still a good idea to use it as a checklist. In this vein, it can be used as written evidence for establishing the tax basis of a capital asset at time of death. When property is acquired from a decedent, its tax basis is "stepped up" (or stepped down) to its fair market value on date of death [IRC §

1014(a)(1)]. Said basis then becomes the tax reference for determining gain or loss when the asset is sold or exchanged subsequent to death. In what form is this written evidence preserved?

Answer: By a professionally prepared third-party statement such as—

VERIFICATION: NO FORM 706 REQUIRED

Said verification statement summarizes from Form 706 all assets of the decedent and lists each asset's fair market value. The verification also summarizes all debts and liabilities that are subject to discharge, before the decedent's property can be distributed to others.

Having a verification accounting document at hand is just what every executor needs, when responding to questions and criticisms from distributees. The gross estate **minus** all debts, expenses, fees, and taxes is that which is distributable. All recipients thereof (including the trustee of the decedent's trust) receive their share of said property free and clear of all applicable tax and debt. This enables each distributee to make a *fresh start* for his own accounting needs. Recall Figure 6.1.

Income Transition Form 1041

Despite our portrayal in Figure 6.1, the role of an executor is not quite done. He must see to it that Form 1040: *U.S. Individual Income Tax Return*, is finalized and submitted to the IRS. If the decent was single, there must be a final Form 1040. If the decedent was married, there must be a final joint Form 1040. The word "Final" has to be printed on the top of the return, followed by the deceased taxpayer's date of death.

After death, income may be, and often is, generated by the assets of the decedent. If so, there is Form 1041 to be addressed. It is helpful to think of the last digit "1" as meaning "after death." There are two versions of Form 1041: an *estate* version and, separately, a *trust* version (if a trust is indeed applicable). We call Form 1041 the *income transition* form. The estate version covers the income transition from the date of death to close out of the decedent's estate. The trust version covers the income transition from date of transfer from the estate version throughout the duration of the trust, until its termination. These two versions of the same tax form constitute two separate income accounting roles. In Figure 6.3, we portray the more difficult estate accounting role. Once this is done, the trust accounting begins (via Form 1041).

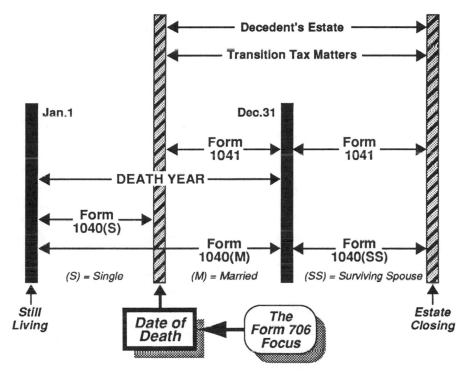

Fig. 6.3 - Transition Tax Forms When a Testator Dies

Most unfortunately, the title of Form 1041 is identical, whether an estate or a trust is involved. Its official title is: *U.S. Income Tax Return for Estates and Trusts*. It is the word "and" that makes it an unfortunate title. The word "and" gives the impression that the reporting of income from the estate of a decedent and reporting the income from the trust of a decedent are concurrent. This is NOT the case. The two Forms 1041 are sequential. The estate version has to be finalized before the trust version commences. The Form 1041

LIVING WILLS & TRUSTS

preparer signals to the IRS the distinction by X-ing the appropriate checkboxes: ☐ Estate; ☐ Trust; ☐ Initial; ☐ Final.

The distinction is also made by the use of separate Tax ID numbers, called: EINs (Employer Identification Number). An official EIN is obtained for the estate; a different EIN is obtained for the trust. IRS Form SS-4 (*Application for* . . .) is used for these purposes. The executor applies for the estate EIN; the trustee applies for the trust EIN. Once the estate is closed, the trust, where applicable, takes off on its own.

Identification Duty of Trustee

When a husband and wife create a trust while both are alive, the trust document is revocable. This means that the trust as an operational entity is dormant. It is activated only after the first trustor-spouse dies. Even then it is only partially activated: that portion of the property belonging to the deceased spouse. The trustee must identify all elements of the trustor's property, and distinguish between those items which go into the irrevocable portion of the trust, and those which remain in the revocable portion. This separation and identity of trust properties is no easy task.

In California, for example, CPC § 16009 states that:

The trustee has a duty—

(a)   To keep the trust property separate from other property not subject to the trust.

(b)   To see that the trust property is designated as property of the trust.

This duty is exacerbated when the trust instrument calls for rearranging the trust property of the first decedent into one or more subtrusts. The number of subtrusts depends upon the gross value of the trust estate. A $10 to $20 million trust estate would have more subtrusts than a $1 to $2 million trust.

If the decedent's distributable-to-trust estate is less than the Form 706 filing thresholds previously given, only one subtrust would be involved. This would likely be: *Subtrust A* or *Exempt*. It is "exempt" because assets in this subtrust would bypass inclusion in the surviving trustor's estate when that trustor dies.

With respect to married trustors, if the first decedent's estate is large enough, a *Marital Deduction Trust* (subtrust B) invariably would be indicated. This subtrust gets its name from Schedule M of Form 706: *Bequests, etc. to Surviving Spouse* [IRC Sec. 2056]. Whatever the amount of this bequest is, it is deductible against the first decedent's taxable estate. It is so, because the unconsumed portion of it is a required inclusion in the second deceased spouse's estate. This exclusion-inclusion feature enables the surviving spouse to have access to the Schedule M amount, consume it as necessary, and pay death tax on the residual portion (since it was not taxed in the first decedent's estate). The separation, identifying, and subtrusting of the Schedule M assets is one of the most difficult duties of a family member trustee. We try to portray this difficulty in Figure 6.4.

Still, other subtrusts could be involved. There could be a charitable remainder subtrust (Schedule O of Form 706), a generation-skipping subtrust (Schedule R of Form 706), a family-owned business subtrust (Schedule T of Form 706), a conservation easement subtrust (Schedule U of Form 706), and/or one or more special needs subtrusts not recognized on Form 706. Each of these subtrusts is a separate tax accounting entity of its own.

Trustee as "Investment Manager"

Once trust property is separated and identified (subtrusts A and B above, for example), it comes under the exclusive dominion and control of the trustee. The question then arises: What does the trustee do with the trust property?

Answer: Unless the property is to be distributed immediately, it is invested. It is invested with the intent of generating income for the beneficiaries and for, hopefully, "growing" the initial trust principal through appreciation. The intent also is to preserve the principal for periodic distributions per instructions in the trust instrument. This means that the trustee must engage in business-type transactions: buying, selling, exchanging, modifying, etc. In

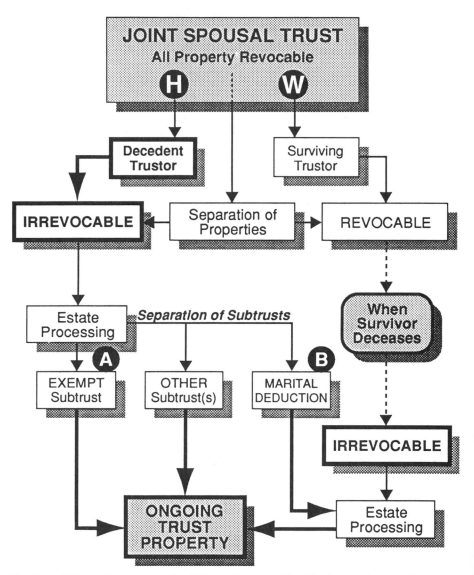

Fig. 6.4 - "Exclusion - Inclusion" Care Required for Marital Deduction Property

doing so, ordinary business risks are at stake. There are downside potentials as well as upside potentials for such risks.

What every trustee fears most is that the initial trust principal may indeed *depreciate* in value. If this happens, the trustee is subjected to beneficiary-perceived acts of mishandling trust assets. To protect the trustee against unwarranted accusations, most states' trust codes impose a standard-of-care rule on the trustee.

In California, for example, the statutory standard-of-care is set forth in CPC § 16040. This section reads in part as—

(a)   The trustee shall administer the trust with care, skill, prudence, and diligence **under the circumstances then prevailing** *that a prudent person acting in a like capacity and familiar with such matters would use in the conduct of an enterprise of like character and with like aims to accomplish the purposes of the trust* **as determined from the trust instrument**. [Emphasis added.]

This "prudent person" theme is expanded on by CPC § 16047 for investments and management. This section reads in part as—

(c)   Among the circumstances that are appropriate to consider in investing and managing trust assets are the following:

(1)   General economic conditions.
(2)   The possible effect of inflation or deflation.
(3)   The expected tax consequences.
(4)   The expected total return from income and the appreciation of capital.
(5)   Needs for liquidity, regularity of income, and preservation of capital.

In the real world, if an investment turns sour, hindsight brings out the worst in people. In the case of a trust, some beneficiaries get angry and threaten lawsuits against the trustee. In defense, the trustee must show that he acted in good faith and with due diligence and care at all times.

Annual Use of Form 1041

One of the best protections of a trustee is his dutifully filing each year IRS Form 1041: *U.S. Income Tax Return for . . . Trusts*.

Each said return has a box on its page 1 for entering the number of beneficiaries having a financial interest in the trust. For each such beneficiary, a Schedule K-1 (Form 1041): **Beneficiary's Share of Income, Deductions, Credits, etc.**, is prepared. Attached to each Schedule K-1, the trustee can attach his own formatted: *Report of Account.*

As pursuant to CPC § 16063, the contents of each report of account shall consist of the following (with emphasis added):

*(1) A statement of **receipts and disbursements** of principal and income that have occurred during the last complete fiscal year of the trust or since the last account.*

*(2) A statement of the **assets and liabilities** of the trust as of . . . the end of the period covered by the account.*

*(3) The **trustee's compensation** [and expenses] . . . since the last account.*

*(4) The **agents hired** by the trustee, their relationship to the trustee, if any, and their compensation.*

*(5) A statement that the recipient of the account may **petition the court** . . . to obtain a court review of the account and of the acts of the trustee.*

*(6) A statement that **claims against the trustee** for breach of trust may not be made after the expiration of **three years** from the date the beneficiary receives an account or report disclosing facts giving rise to the claim.*

A prudent trustee tries to go along with the wishes of the beneficiaries as much as he can. But he is not beholden to them with regard to their every suggestion for investments, accounting procedures, and the use of agents by the trust. In fact, one of his duties is **not** to delegate to anyone that which he can reasonably do on his own. [CPC § 16012.]

7

OTHER LIVING OPTIONS

During-Life Transfers Of Property For No Consideration In Money Or Money's Worth Are NONTESTAMENTARY By Nature. As Such, They Avoid Probate And The Interpretative Ambiguities Of Wills And Trusts. By Far, The Most Practical Arrangement Is JOINT TENANCY With Right Of Survivorship. Joint Tenancy, However, Does NOT Avoid Tax Reporting Rules At Time Of Death. Other Nontestamentary Transfers Include Retained Life Estates, Annual Exclusion Gifts, Larger Gifts Up To $1,000,000 (1 million) Cumulatively, Taxable Gifts Via IRS Form 709, Powers Of Attorney, And Powers Of Appointment (When Contemplating Death).

Yes. There are other ways to transfer property, gratuitously, while the transferor is alive. These options are called: *nontestamentary* transfers. They take effect during life rather than upon death. Because the transfer of ownership takes effect during life, no probate proceedings whatsoever are required. The presumption is that the transferor knows what he is doing and why. If, for some reason, a dispute arises concerning a transfer, the living person making the transfer is available for interrogation. For small-to-modest estates, living transfers can substitute quite well for wills and trusts. For large estates, living transfers can augment testamentary dispositions.

By far the most common living transfer of ownership is joint tenancy. That is, the owner-transferor simply adds another person's name to the ownership of his property. He wouldn't do this with a stranger, of course, but certainly with members of his own family. For example, a widow parent adds the name of her adult daughter to the parent's home, to the parent's bank account, to the parent's stock fund, and to any other item in which the parent has some form of ownership interest. When the parent dies, the property passes to the daughter . . . by operation of state law.

Accordingly, in this chapter, we want to explain the various options you have for transferring ownership interests in property to others, while you are alive. Our focus is strictly on those transfers to family members, close and dear friends, and to others who merit your generosity for higher education, disability needs, and elder care services. With or without a will, or with or without a trust, there are times when other persons' needs cannot wait for your death. Transfers to purely charitable organizations (for which you get tax deductions) are beyond the scope of our discussion.

Joint Tenancy: WROS

The letters "WROS" stand for: **W**ith **R**ight **O**f **S**urvivorship. This means that if a property item shows that two or more persons own it, and one of them dies, the surviving joint tenant(s) become the owner(s) thereof. No probate is required to authenticate the surviving tenant's (or tenants') ownership. This is by operation of state law where the joint tenancy arrangement was made. The arrangement is simply a matter of adding a name to an existing property item. No money needs to change hands. The process is practical and convenient where family members are the names being added.

With joint tenancy property, only one instrument is needed to describe the property. Once multiple names are shown on the instrument, all co-tenants have equal rights to share in the use and enjoyment of the item during their lives. On the death of a joint tenant, the property descends to the survivor or survivors and at length to the last survivor.

In the case of real property, the clause: "With right of survivorship," is added to the joint tenancy title. A title to real property is called a *deed*. It is a written instrument recorded in the county where the real land is geographically located. For example, a father might add his son's name as—

John J. Jones, father, and Timothy M. Jones, his son, as joint tenants WROS.

The instrument could be a Joint Tenancy Deed, a Quitclaim Deed, a Gift Deed Joint Tenancy, or some other variant depending on local custom. Because local custom prevails, we urge the engagement of a local real estate attorney for preparing the new title documentation, when adding a name gratuitously to any parcel of realty. In such cases, full legal description of the property must be cited.

In the adding-a-name example above, note the connective word "and" in the title. This is because all joint tenants must co-sign simultaneously before the realty can be subsequently sold or exchanged. The ownership of a parcel of land is generally regarded as "undivided" property. This means that one can add names, but no single name can sell or exchange the property without full consent of the others.

The adding-name(s) situation is quite different for nonrealty assets: bank accounts, certificates of deposit, investment accounts, mutual funds, vehicles, equipment, etc. In these cases, each co-ownership name is separated from the other with the conjunctive: "or" (meaning: either . . . or). For example—

John J. Jones or Timothy M. Jones or Patricia (Jones) White.

The word "or" enables any one of the joint tenants to access the account(s) — for individual use or consumption — without consent of other joint tenants. This is because said account(s) can be incrementally consumed as need be. A parcel of real estate cannot be similarly consumed.

How many names can be added gratuitously to an owner's real property and/or to monetary accounts? Theoretically, any number. But, practically, we think the number is three: certainly no more than four. The more the number of co-tenants, the finer the slicing of share fractions [50% (for 2), 33 1/3% (for 3), 25% (for 4), 20% (for 5), etc.]. The number is set by the primary owner.

Probate Avoidance Only

The "right of survivorship" via joint tenancy is strictly a convenient probate avoidance arrangement. It does nothing to avoid death tax considerations when one of the co-tenants dies. Suppose, for example, a widower (father) adds the name of his son and his daughter to the title to his personal residence (valued at $660,000). Shortly thereafter, the son is killed in an auto accident. How much is included in the son's estate for death tax consideration purposes?

Answer: $220,000 ($660,000 ÷ 3). Yet, the son contributed no money when his name was added to the property title. In reality, he is a beneficial owner: not an economic owner. So, if the father can show that the son contributed no money, there would be no inclusion in the son's estate.

Now, suppose the father died. How much of the $660,000 property value would be includible in his estate for death tax purposes: $220,000?

No. Since the father is the true economic owner of his residence, the entire $660,000 would be included in his estate. His son and daughter would inherit the residence co-equally as surviving joint tenants . . . without probate, without a will, and without a trust.

This one feature alone makes joint tenancy a popular arrangement among family members. Probate avoidance takes precedence over death tax avoidance. This is especially true today when the death tax exclusion amounts are $1,500,000 (1.5 million) for death years 2004 and 2005; $2,000,000 (2 million) for death years 2006 through 2008; and $3,500,000 (3.5 million) for death years 2009 and thereafter. For the average family with a modest estate, joint tenancy is clearly the way to go.

When a particular estate exceeds the thresholds above, and there are joint tenancy arrangements, the general inclusion rule applies. This rule, espoused in the instructions to Schedule E (Form 706): *Jointly Owned Property*, reads in part as—

> *Generally, you must include the full value of the jointly owned property . . . unless you can show that any part of the property was acquired with consideration originally belonging to the surviving joint tenant or tenants.*

Some Practical Examples

A mother with two adult children decides to add her two children's names to her various bank accounts, money market accounts, and other investment accounts. She does so "for convenience only." She wants the children to have access to her funds in the event of her sickness, injury, senility, or death. Each child has withdrawal authority only with consent of the mother while she is alive. This is good financial disciplining by the mother. When the mother dies, there is no question that 100% of the joint tenancy property is includible in her gross estate. Neither child made any contributory interests in money or money's worth.

Here's another common case. A father with three adult children acquired from his parents an 8-unit apartment complex which was rented. Although his spouse was alive, the rental complex was not marital property: it was inherited. For convenience only, the father added the three children's names to the property deed. He had the title re-recorded as joint tenants with right of survivorship. All three children worked on the property and helped to mange and maintain it. Each year, the father gave each child a computer-generated "Gift Certificate" signifying a $10,000 per year contributory ownership interest in the 8-unit rental building. When the father dies, it becomes a matter of reconstructing each child's ownership interest in cumulative money and money's worth. In the end, however, no matter what each child's reconstructed interests might be, the IRS would insist that at least 25% of the property's value $(1 \div 4)$ be included in the father's gross estate. Conceivably, it might insist on more than 25% being includible.

In another case, an unmarried man and an unmarried woman lived together. They lived in her house which was worth about $500,000. He had a commercial fishing boat and license worth about $285,000. They each kept their own separate bank accounts. However, they pooled together all of their investment money (totaling $365,000) into one growth stock mutual fund. Both names were shown on the account as joint tenants and co-owners. On one of his regular fishing trips, the male co-owner was swept overboard in a violent storm and drowned. His two crew members recovered the body and returned the boat to port. What portion of the

$365,000 co-owned investment account is includible in the decedent's estate (whether or not death taxed)?

Answer: $365,000 . . . plus growth in the account ($50,000 say) to date of death. A lower amount would be included if the monetary contribution of the decedent could be established with certainty. After exhaustively tracing the various pre-pooled accounts of the decedent, his initial contributory share was determined to be $160,000. With this information, the decedent's percentage includible would be:

$$160,000 \div 365,000 = 43.83\% \text{ or } 0.4383$$

The includible value at date of death would be—

$$[365,000 + 50,000] \times 0.4838 = \$197,673.$$

Added to this $197,673 would be the decedent's fishing boat ($285,000) plus (most likely) 50% of his unmarried partner's $500,000 residence (or $250,000). Altogether, his gross estate inclusion amount would total $732,673. If his partner's residence were placed in joint tenancy (for convenience in the event of her death), the grand total estate inclusion would be $982,673. This is still below the death tax exclusion amounts.

Our point is this. If there is a practical convenience benefit for joint tenancy ownership of property, by all means pursue it. Often, it is better to make such transfers during life rather than waiting for death and its attendant interpretation uncertainties with wills and trusts. One has to plan for living, as well as for death.

Retained Life Estate

There is another form of during-life transfer which is not as common, nor as well understood, as joint tenancy arrangements. This is the process called: *Retained life estate.* A life estate is where legal title to property is transferred, but the right to use the property is retained by the transferor or until his death. That is, the full title is complete, but the transfer of full possession is incomplete. Upon death of the transferor, full possession passes to the transferee.

The life estate concept is particularly attractive to an elderly parent (widow or widower) who wants to stay in his or her home, without fear of being forced out by covetous adult children. At the same time, the parent has increasing need for income and support. Medical bills, hospital stays, and prescription medication keep always escalating. Under the retained life-use concept, the parent can sell part of her house, and retain part.

Think of one's home, if you will, as two legally/actuarially separate pieces of property. One piece is a "life interest"; this is the portion that the parent retains. The other piece is the "remainder interest"; this is the portion that the parent can sell. Each piece is actuarially and statistically defined as a fraction to five decimal places. The five fractions must add up to 100%. For example, suppose the life interest fraction were 0.63743; the remainder fraction would be 0.36257 (1.00000 − 0.63743 = 0.36257).

IRC Section 7520: *Valuation Tables*, requires the IRS to publish every 10 years statistical tables for determining—

the value of any annuity, any interest for life or a term of years, or any remainder or reversionary interest.

The most recent tables were published in 1999 and are applicable through 2009. For illustration purposes, we have selected IRS Table S (7.2). We present it to you in Figure 7.1 in abbreviated form. The "S" stands for single life. The "7.2" relates to the Federal mid-term rate of interest (which changes every month) for the month in which the valuation date falls. The term "valuation date" refers to the fair market value of property (usually real estate) when its life estate value is to be determined.

Thus, for any given age, one's life interest and remainder interest in his home (or other real property) can be officially determined. Suppose, for example, that at age 70, your widowed mother's home is worth $850,000. She needs additional money for income and support, but she does not want to leave her home. With a retained life estate therein, she could sell the remainder fraction (0.43626 from Figure 7.1) for $370,820 ($850,000 x 0.43626). This amount of money would surely provide for additional needs. Make sure you engage an elder-care attorney to oversee the sale.

IRS TABLE S (7.2)					
Based on Mortality Table 90 CM Through 2009					
Age	Life Estate	Remainder	Age	Life Estate	Remainder
50	0.81195	0.18805	75	0.48523	0.51477
55	0.76147	0.23853	80	0.40235	0.59765
60	0.70301	0.29699	85	0.32170	0.67830
65	0.63743	0.36257	90	0.24779	0.75221
70	0.56374	0.43626	95	0.19039	0.80961

Fig. 7.1 - Example Actuarial Fractions for Single Life Estates

A retained-life-estate sale creates a "restricted title" for the buyer. He cannot resell the property until the life tenant either consents voluntarily or deceases. So, who would buy a personal residence with a life tenant living in it?

Only family members would likely buy it. The more likely ones would be those who would inherit the property anyhow. Even if one, two, or three members could not scrape up $370,820 in cash, they could offer to buy on an installment-sale arrangement. The parent would then be the mortgage holder and would receive monthly payments (principal *and* interest) until she died. If she died at age 90, for example, the amount includible in her gross estate for death tax consideration purposes would be 0.24779 (or about 25%) of the home's appraised value at that time. There likely would be no death tax whatsoever. The heirs would receive the property free and clear: no probate, no will, no trust.

Annual Exclusion Gifts

If the commitment of money or property via joint tenancy or life estate is not palatable, the idea of making small annual gifts could be. By "small" we mean: around $10,000 or so. If no strings are attached, the gifts can be made annually to any number of donees (recipients), without concern for any form of transfer or gift tax. Since there is a gift tax "out there" [IRC Sec. 2501(a): *Taxable Transfers*], the annual exclusion transfers are referred to as *nontaxable gifts*. The primary condition for nontaxability is that the donor (the giver) sever all dominion and control over the gifted property. This severance enables the donee to spend the money or sell the property as he or she sees fit.

The annual exclusion amount is set forth in IRC Section 2503(b): *Taxable Gifts; Exclusions from Gifts*. The basic amount is $10,000 . . . adjusted for inflation for years after 1998. As of the year 2004, the inflation adjusted exclusion amount was $11,000. There is no limit to the number of years, nor is there any limit to number of donees each year to whom the exclusion gifts can be made. This "no limit" feature allows the donor wide discretion in how much money or property he gifts away each year. The general concept involved is depicted in Figure 7.2.

Where gifts are made to an educational institution or to a medical facility on behalf of a designated student or patient, the $10,000 (or so) annual limit does not apply [IRC Sec. 2503(e)]. This means that a donor can sponsor one or more students each year (most likely within his own family circle) for each student's education program of choice. Similarly for medical patients.

If the annual gifting is made directly to a person under the age of 21, the gifted amount each year can be set aside into a custodial account. This is called a *Gift to Minors* account [IRC Sec. 2503(c)]. Usually, the parent of the child (who is **not** the donor) is the assigned custodian. The idea is to enable the donor (most likely a grandparent) to make repeated annual exclusion gifts where the minor does not have immediate access to the cumulative buildup of money . . . which surely would be needed later.

If a grandparent started giving $10,000 (plus inflation adjustment) to a grandchild when one year old, by the time the child reached age 21, nearly $250,000 (approximately 1/4 million dollars) would be available. Releasing this amount of money to a 21-year-old is NOT the prudent thing to do. Just before the 21-year-age date, the custodian (depending on local practice) could set up a *spendthrift* investment/savings account that would limit the magnitude of withdrawals each year. It could be some form of spendthrift trust into which continuing annual exclusion gifts could be made. Such gifts could continue until the "protected person" attained a specified age representing *financial maturity*. Often, age 35 is cited for this purpose.

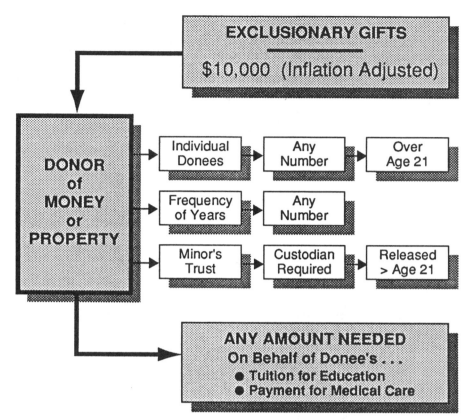

Fig. 7.2 - Exclusions From Taxable Gifts: The Essentials

Larger Gifts Permitted

It is not that one cannot gift more than $10,000 (inflation adjusted). It is that any amount in excess of the annual exclusion is taxable. Suppose, for example, that one gave to a needy member of his family a single premium lifetime annuity of $110,000. Of this amount, $100,000 would be a taxable gift and $10,000 would be excluded as nontaxable. But under current rules, even the $100,000 taxable is **not actually taxed!** Does this make sense?

No; it does not make sense if all you have to go on is what we've just given you. But it does make sense when we tell you that there is a *one-time cumulative gift tax exclusion* of $1,000,000 (1 million). This cumulative exclusion amount and the annual exclusion amounts are different tax worlds. The cumulative exclusion amount is tracked with IRS Form 709: *U.S. Gift Tax Return* (more on this later), whereas there is no IRS tracking whatsoever of the annual nontaxable gifts.

With the help of Figure 7.3, perhaps we can explain the situation a little better. The federal tax code does not use the term: "one-time cumulative gift tax exclusion." Instead, it uses the more obfuscating term: *Unified Credit Against Gift Tax* [IRC Section 2505]. For years through 2009, IRS subsection 2505(a) reads, in part, as—

There shall be allowed as a credit against the tax imposed by Section 2501 [Imposition of Gift Tax] *for each calendar year an amount equal to—*

(1) *the applicable credit amount . . . (determined as if the* *applicable exclusion amount* *were $1,000,000), reduced by*

(2) *the sum of the amounts* *allowable as a credit . . . for* *all preceding calendar periods.* [Emphasis added.]

We read this statutory wording as one exclusion amount of $1,000,000 reduced by all prior credits towards that one amount. Thus, if you add up all prior allowable exclusion credits cumulatively, you cannot exceed $1,000,000 that is not taxed. Any amount over $1,000,000 is gift taxed at a rate between 35% and 45%, depending on the extent of overage. We doubt that many readers of this book would have the wherewithal to give more than $1,000,000 cumulatively to one or more family members while alive. Since a gift made during life is a gift, it is not subject to probate, nor to the interpretation of a will, nor to the provisions of a noncharitable trust.

Tracking Taxable Gifts

In general, the gift tax rates are higher than ordinary income tax rates. Because so, the IRS is not going to let a prosperous donor gift away large sums of money without the IRS knowing about it. If a large gift is made to a charitable entity, the IRS will know about

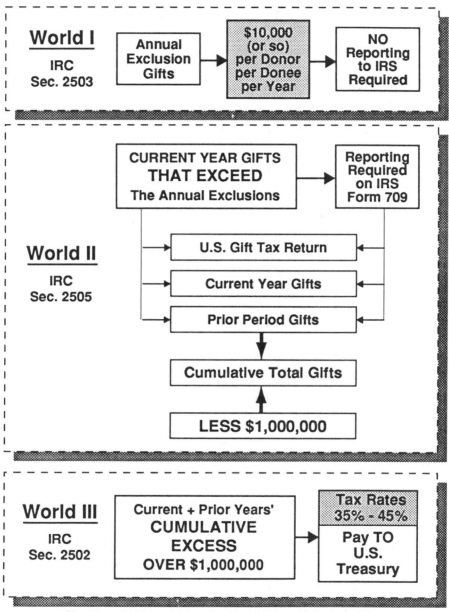

Fig. 7.3 - Distinguishing the Taxability of Lifetime Gifts

it almost immediately. This is because the donor will claim an income tax deduction for it. But if a large gift — say, for example, $600,000 — were made to a family member, there would be no income tax deduction to the donor. And because the $600,000 gift is less than $1,000,000, the donor would pay no gift tax. So, how is the IRS going to know about the $600,000 family gift?

Answer: Two ways. A back-handed way or an upfront way. First, the back-handed way.

Suppose the $600,000 were used for the cash purchase of a desperately needed home by the family member. Taxwise, no report by the donee family member is necessary. It was a pure gift. How lucky can a family member be?

But, suppose that the title company closing the purchase was a little uneasy about payment in full, with a "pay to" personal check. If so, the title company would call in its attorney who might ask a series of intimidating questions of the donee-buyer. The line of questioning might imply that the gift money might have arisen from some illicit drug operation, or from some money-laundering scheme, or from some offshore tax shelter. Such a line of questioning might frighten the donee to the point where he (or she) agrees to report the $600,000 as income on Form 1040 as "Other income." This satisfies the title company, and the deal closes.

The "Other income" line on Form 1040 is *line 21: Other income. List type and amount.* The donee-buyer enters in the indicated white spaces: *Gift of $600,000;* taxable amount -0- (for zero). When the IRS's computer processing notes this entry, it will ignore the zero and tax in full the $600,000. It will send a change notice to the donee-buyer-taxpayer permitting that person to contest the IRS's proposed additional tax. Instructions require that the taxpayer supply all particulars.

One particular item the IRS would want is the donor's full name and social security number (SSN). With such information, the IRS would search its data bank to see if the donor had filed **Form 709:** *U.S. Gift Tax Return.* This would be the upfront way for reporting the $600,000 gift. Even more upfront would be for the donor to give the donee a photocopy of the filed Form 709. Showing a copy to the title company and its attorney (in the example above) should allay any skepticism concerning origin of the gift.

Grant of Certain Powers

Another approach to transfers during life could be the grant of certain powers to designated family members. The term "grant of power" means that the owner of money or property can grant (allow) some nonowner (the grantee) the right to access and use the money or property for the grantee's own self benefit. If the total value of money and property available for such grant is less than $1,000,000 (1 million), the gift rules of Figure 7.3 apply.

One of the simplest grant-of-powers arrangements is the use of credit cards or debit cards. The owner (parent, grandparent, uncle/aunt) "loans" a credit card or a debit card to one or more family members. Each grantee can use the card (for his/her own purposes) until the set limits are reached: $5,000; $10,000; or whatever. When the limits are reached, they are either renewed, or suspended for awhile, then renewed.

Another form of grant is: *general power of attorney.* A "power of attorney" is a notarized document which authorizes an agent for the grantor to perform business-type tasks. Preprinted general-power-of-attorney forms are available commercially. The preprinted wording includes such language as—

> . . . *the authority and power to make, endorse, cash, and negotiate checks, other evidences of indebtedness, . . . and to sell, convey, mortgage, deed in trust, lease, and otherwise deal with property of every kind, whether real, personal, tangible, or intangible . . . .*

There is also what is called a *General power of appointment.* This is the granting of power to access, control, and/or consume one's property in anticipation of his (the grantor's) death. The granting can be done by a legal instrument. The grantee has the right to exercise the power in favor of himself or his creditors. When so exercisable, the power is treated as a transfer of property from the grantor/testator/trustor to the possessor. The possessor thereafter has to include such power as his own property at the time of his/her demise.

8

KNOWING YOUR PROPERTY

> Not All Testators Are As Familiar With Their Property Holdings As They Should Be. Said Property Is That Which Is Real, Tangible, Intangible, Or Personal WHEREVER SITUATED (Whether Within Or Without the U.S.). When A Person Dies, The IRS Seeks Resurrection Of His Property Into 9 Specific Schedules, Namely: A - Real Estate; B - Stocks & Bonds; C - Mortgages, Notes, & Cash; D - Life Insurance; E - Jointly Owned Items; F - Other Miscellany; G - Transfers During Life; H - Powers Of Appointment; And I - Annuities. When Totaled, And Authorized Subtractions Made, What Is Left Is Distributable To Heirs And Kin.

The underlying purpose of any testamentary instrument is to dispose of one's property upon his demise. One can only direct the disposition of his own property. He cannot direct the disposition of someone else's property, even though it may be his spouse's. Consequently, every testator must declare what property is his own and must identify it with reasonable certainty.

The dictionary defines "property" as *something owned or possessed*: something to which a person has legal title. Ownership of property implies the right to use it, alter it, enjoy it, trade it, or dispose of it as the owner sees fit. Said property may be of various physical forms held in various ownership arrangements and situated nearby or distant to the domicile of the testator. For these and other reasons, a clear knowledge of one's property is essential to the effective distribution of it via his or her will or trust.

The timespan between preparing one's testamentary intentions and his demise is uncertain, and — hopefully — extended. During this timespan numerous property changes can occur. Financial needs change, ownership interests change, new opportunities arise, old opportunities fade, property custodianships change, returns on investments change, and so on. Consequently, rather than declaring an inventory of your property at the time of preparing your will or trust, it is more practical that the declaration be semi-specific and semi-general. This permits flexibility for changing property arrangements without the necessity for changing your testamentary instrument every time you change an item of property.

Accordingly, in this chapter, we want to acquaint you more fully with the four general classes of property holdings you may have: real, tangible, intangible, and personal. We want to examine specifically what each class is comprised of, and extend our examination to the expected tax listings should your executor be required to file IRS Form 706: *U.S. Estate (Transfer) Tax Return* on your behalf. By our doing this, you will know that that which the IRS considers to be "property" extends beyond one's ordinary knowledge in everyday life. Problems with the co-ownership of property are addressed, as well as those problems associated with a multiplicity of portfolio assets, collectibles, and compiling prior-to-death transfers. Knowing your property is more than knowing where your bank account is, the address of your home, the name of your business (if any), and who your investment broker is. Indeed, knowing these and other aspects of your property demonstrates quite fully your testamentary capacity.

Realty and Personalty

Going back into history for a moment, the earliest concept of "property" originated from land. Before the year 1000 A.D., ownership of land was the basis of all power and privilege: socially, politically, militarily, and governmentally. Under both Roman and English law, he who owned land was a sovereign in his own right.

Land was considered to be fixed, immovable, and permanent. He who took physical possession of it, by whatever means, owned it. Because of its immovability, it was *real*: real power, real privilege. All other forms of property related to land in a secondary and subservient way.

Under Roman law, there were just two forms of property: land and movables. Under English law, there also were just two forms of property: land and chattels. As Roman and English law merged, all property became classed as either real property or personal property: realty or personalty. The property concepts of realty and personalty prevailed for centuries.

As property laws became formalized, ownership of realty was identified through deeds and titles. Ownership of personalty was simply a matter of physical possession. Titles to realty were recorded, whereas ownership of personalty was not recorded. Personalty could be transformed, abandoned, or destroyed, whereas realty could not.

From these two divergent concepts of property, a broad middle-ground of property forms evolved. Bridging from realty there arose improvements to land (fixed, semi-fixed, non-fixed) and leaseholds (contractual rights to use the land). Bridging from personalty there arose chattels in possession (tangible movables) and chattels in action (intangibles with legal rights of action). As society became more complex, the distinction between realty and personalty became "spread apart." Interspersed between these two ancient forms, the flexible roles of tangible and intangible property grew.

Four Classes Defined

In modern life, particularly in the 2000s, power and privilege are no longer epitomized in land alone. The main reason for this is the increasing role of Big Government in the United States. In the original founding and early stages of development of this country, jurisdiction of all land vested primarily in the separate states: *not* in the federal government. Today, however, the federal government owns increasingly larger and larger portions of land, and controls virtually all land through various tax laws and regulations, environmental restrictions, and road-building priorities. Consequently, the private ownership of vast acreages of land is rapidly becoming a rare form of property these days. In its place, however, tangible and intangible forms of property abound.

Today, there are four distinct classes of property which a testator may own. These classes are—

Real property
Tangible property
Intangible property
Personal effects

A brief description of each of these four classes is instructive for readying one when preparing his will or trust.

Real property consists of parcels of land with or without fixed structures thereon. The term "fixed structures" means buildings which are anchored to the land by foundations of brick, concrete, wood, and/or steel. Improvements to land such as roadways, utility lines, irrigation systems, sign posts, fences, trees, sidewalks, and the like also are real property. Although they are not anchored with concrete and steel, they are not movable in the everyday sense. Real property, therefore, consists of land, improvements to land, and structures thereon.

Tangible property consists of objects which can be seen, felt, lifted, and moved. The dictionary defines tangible as that which *can be perceived* . . . especially by the sense of touch. Also, tangible property is that which is "capable of being precisely realized by the mind." In the tangible category are vehicles, machinery, equipment, tools, collections (coins, stamps, jewelry, clocks, guns), antiques (furniture, cars), works of art (paintings, sculptures, ceramics), precious metals and stones, minerals, oil and gas, and so on.

Intangible property is that which is incapable of being felt by touch: that which is not readily discerned by the mind. Intangible property is not corporeal; that is, it has no physical body form and therefore is not accompanied by physical possession. It is primarily a *contractual right*. The document or thing representing the contractual right has no intrinsic value of its own. Intangible property, therefore, comprises a wide range of "pieces of paper" rather than actual physical objects.

The classical example of intangible property is so-called "cash." Cash is a monetary instrument protected by legal-tender laws and popularly known as "greenbacks." All U.S. greenbacks are figures printed on pieces of paper. They have no intrinsic value of their own. Whether one has a $1 bill, a $100 bill, or a $1,000 bill, the cost of the paper and the printing is the same: about two cents. These green pieces of paper have legal tender value and are enforceable as monetary instruments only. They are not tangible money in the form of gold or silver.

Similarly, other forms of intangible property are stock certificates, bond certificates, trust deeds, promissory notes, commercial paper, wraparound mortgages, warehouse receipts, mutual fund accounts, checking accounts, savings accounts and so on. All these are pieces of paper representing dollar figures in books of account. An impressive amount of wealth can be accounted for via intangible property.

Personal effects are items, both tangible and intangible, which primarily have *memory value*. They have little or no market value or monetary value. Their memory value is important to heirs, next of kin, close friends, and business associates. Personal effects are of little interest to estate-taxing authorities.

Personal effects include such items and sundries as clothing, memoirs, letters, diaries, ordinary furniture and furnishings, home-made objects, personal handicrafts, hobbies, flowers, and so on. These are the classical items for inclusion in a holographic supplement to your prepared will. Rarely is there any need to include mention of personal effects in your formally prepared will or trust. They have personal value, but no — or nil — market value.

Specific examples of each class of property are presented in Figure 8.1. The listings are a general summarization of the range of property forms that you might have. Do you really know which you have, and which you do not have?

Separate Ownership of Property

The existence of property in any class necessarily involves ownership of that property. It may be owned separately (by one person), jointly (by two persons), or severally (by three or more persons). The simplest form, of course, is separate ownership of property. Separate ownership is that which is in the name or possession of the testator only. Other than purely personal effects,

CATEGORY of PROPERTY			
Real	**Tangible**	**Intangible**	**Personal**
Land	Autos	Stocks & bonds	Clothing
Buildings	Boats	Promissory notes	Artifacts
Roadways	Trailers	Trust deeds	Memoirs
Utility lines	Campers	Commercial paper	Photo albums
Fences & corrals	Airplanes	Bank accounts	Sports equipment
Sign posts	Machinery	Mutual funds	Furniture
Natural resources	Equipment	Cash	• ordinary
Shorefronts	Computers	• greenbacks	Linens & supplies
Waterways	Furniture	Judgements	• household
Mountain areas	Fixtures	Accounts	Utensils
Mines & caves	FAX & phones	• receivable	• kitchen
Farms	Gold & silver	Insurance	Travel gear
Life Estates	Antiques	Goodwill	Souvenirs
	Collections	Damage claims	
	• guns & swords	Tax refunds	
	• stamps & clocks	Compensation	
	Works of art	• post mortem	
	Diamonds	Travelers checks	
	Ceramics	Personal checks	
	Silverware	Pensions	
	China	Annuities	

Fig. 8.1 - Summarization of Property Interests of a Testator

the separate property of a testator must be clearly distinguished from that which is jointly owned or severally owned.

Separate ownership occurs when one purchases property with his own proceeds, such as with compensation from his personal services or from the sale of previous separate property. Separate property also occurs when one inherits property or is gifted property from someone else. One can also create separate property on his own. He may win it in a lottery or contest or he may find it on his own. Whatever the form of acquisition, separately-owned property is that which either is in the recorded name of the testator only or in his sole physical possession at the time of his demise.

Maintaining separate property identity is frequently difficult. This is particularly true where one has allowed his separate property to be commingled with the separate property of others. This is also true where one has allowed his property to be used over a long period of time for charitable purposes or in the public domain. The commingling of separately-owned property and/or its "loan" to charitable or public institutions must be clarified at the time one prepares his will. Otherwise, interpretive confusion will arise.

Here's the point that we are trying to make: Whenever there is separately-owned property, the testator must clearly establish such ownership in his will or trust. He must carefully define his own part, and identify the part or parts belonging to others.

Husband and Wife Property

A special form of ownership exists between husband and wife. This special ownership derives from English common law which treats married man and woman as a "unity." The common law imposes on each spouse the duty to give each other a "community of life" in company, affection, and service. Thereupon, each is treated equally in his or her right to property acquired during their marriage.

Most forms of property law in the United States seek to reconcile the stability of the household community, the protection of minor children, the interests of the families of both spouses, and the principle of equality of the sexes. These compromising goals are sought via "community property" laws in so-called community states, and via "curtesy and dower" laws in non-community states.

Of the 50 states in the U.S., eight treat the assets acquired by husband and wife as community property. The eight community property states are—

Arizona	Nevada
California	New Mexico
Idaho	Texas
Louisiana	Washington

The community property laws in these eight states are similar but not identical

These states treat *all property* acquired by husband wife during their marriage as belonging one-half to each. This one-half treatment applies regardless of which spouse actually acquired it or from whose funds it was acquired.

Exceptions to the community property rule apply where—

(a)   property was acquired before marriage,
(b)   property is acquired during marriage by inheritance,
(c)   property is acquired during marriage by gift, and
(d)   property is acquired during marriage while domiciled in a non-community state.

These exceptions become the separate property of the relevant spouse, and remain so, so long as it can be separately traced. If separate property between spouses cannot be clearly traced, it is considered commingled and, therefore, community property in community states.

To one degree or another, the non-community-property states achieve the one-half community principle via curtesy and dower laws. Curtesy laws give the husband survivorship interest in the property of his wife, whereas dower laws give the wife survivorship interest in the property of her husband. The non-community-property states differ markedly as to who owns the property during life when acquired by funds earned by one spouse only. In such cases, however, it is usually possible for the property to be acquired in the joint names of the husband and wife as "tenants by the entirety." This ownership form establishes the absolute right of survivorship between spouses.

Because there are more non-community states than community states, federal death tax laws seek to standardize the one-half marital property concept. If a federal death tax applies, there is allowed a "qualified marital interest" *exclusion* in non-community states. The essence of this exclusion is that it permits the decedent spouse's executor to treat one-half of the gross marital estate as belonging to the surviving spouse in his/her own right. Thus, the surviving spouse's one-half is not subject to death tax accounting in the decedent spouse's estate. To get this one-half exclusion, there must be "incidents of common ownership" between the spouses. No exclusion is allowed for separate property of the decedent spouse.

In many marital property cases, there often are separate property aspects to be considered. Among cooperative spouses, that which is 50/50 property should be (more or less) self evident. As to their separate properties, each spouse has the task of tracing his or her own. The overall effort required is depicted in Figure 8.2.

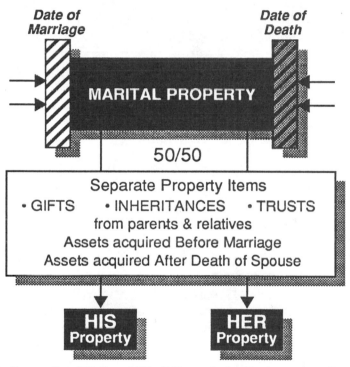

Fig. 8.2 - Separating "His" and "Her" Property for Testamentary Purposes

Joint Tenancy vs. Tenancy in Common

Where *other than spousal property rights* are involved, there are two common forms of co-ownership. These forms are joint tenancy and tenancy in common. In either case, the property is physically *undivided*. As such, each co-owner has the right to possess and the privilege to use the whole thing. Cooperative co-owners are allowed to agree among themselves as to who will have possession in fact, since all have possession in law. If they cannot agree, one or more can petition the court to have the property partitioned among them. It then becomes "divided" property. If actual physical division is impracticable, the court will order the property sold and the proceeds divided among the co-owners.

In cooperative co-ownership cases, the owners have generally agreed among themselves as to their divisional interests. In joint tenancies, the presumption is that all co-owners are co-equal. That is, if there are two joint tenants, each owns 50% of the property. If there are three joint tenants, each owns 33 1/3%; if four joint tenants, each owns 25% . . . and so on. If one of the joint tenants dies, the property interests are re-equalized among the surviving co-owners. Because of this re-equalization, joint tenancy tends to be a *family affair*. When the initial owner dies, his siblings, children, grand-children, etc. seek to divide up the property interests so that each retains his or her "fair share."

In contrast, tenancy in common is more of a *business affair*. At the very outset, each co-owner is expected to contribute a specified amount of money, property, or services to establish his or her ownership interest in the arrangement. Although all co-owners could contribute equally, seldom is this done. When the agreed amount of initial capitalization is acquired, each co-owner's separate fraction (or percentage) can be determined with mathematical precision. The arrangements could be such that, if there were two co-owners, for example, their ownership interests might be 35/65 (35% + 65% = 100%); if three co-owners, their respective interests might be 25/35/40 (25% + 35% + 40% = 100%); if four co-owners, their respective interests might be 15/20/30/35 (15% + 20% + 30% + 35% = 100%) . . . and so on.

The co-ownership fractions (or percentages) can change at any time during the business operation. When this happens, the altered ownership fractions should be confirmed in writing.

Unlike that of joint tenancy, there is no automatic right of survivorship when property is held in tenancy in common. If a co-owner dies, his specific ownership fraction (or percentage) is includible in his gross estate. After inclusion and taxation thereon, the decedent's ownership fraction passes to his heirs or others as directed by his testamentary dispositions.

IRS Property Schedules

Now that we've given you the general idea of property distinctions, the next step is to see how the IRS makes the distinctions. Whereas we have indicated four classes of property, the IRS characterizes property into nine classes! Instead of classes, they are called "schedules" and are so alphabetized on Form 706: *U.S. Estate (Transfer) Tax Return*. While not every property owner who dies will have to prepare IRS Form 706, it is very instructive for you to be aware of such schedules. Upon your death, your executor has to inventory and appraise *all* of your property holdings for various tax purposes. As such, the nine schedules are collectively identified as: *Gross Estate Schedules*. We list all nine for you in Figure 8.3. You should take a moment to at least skim-read down the listing.

Form 706	U.S. Estate Tax Return	
Page 3, Part 5 - Recapitulation		
Schedule	//////////////////////////	Value at Death
//////////	Gross Estate	//////////
A	Real Estate	
B	Stocks & Bonds	
C	Mortgages, Notes, & Cash	
D	Insurance on Decedent's Life	
E	Jointly Owned Property	
F	Other Miscellaneous Property	
G	Transfers During Decedent's Life	
H	Powers of Appointment	
I	Annuities	

Fig. 8.3 - The 9 Gross Estate Schedules on Form 706

Upon doing so, you will note that the very first property characterization therein is **Real Estate** — Schedule A. The instructions to Schedule A (Form 706) require a descriptive listing and the current market value of all parcels of land owned and used by the decedent. On this point, and for all gross estate schedules,

IRC Section 2033 is directly pertinent. The title of Section 2033 is: *Property in Which Decedent Had an Interest*. Its one sentence mandate reads—

> *The value of the gross estate shall include the value of all property* **to the extent of the** [ownership] *interest therein of the decedent at the time of his death.* [Emphasis added.]

By its very nature, land, together with its appurtenances, is subject to co-ownership and multiple ownership arrangements. This characteristic is more prevalent in real estate holdings than with other forms of a decedent's assets. Hence, the ownership aspects of the decedent must be identified in exact percentages of the total parcel, for proper entry on Schedule A. Generally, if the decedent owns 50% or more of a real estate item, that item is entered on Schedule A. If he owns less than 50%, the item is listed and described on other schedules, such as E, F, G, or H.

The official instructions to Schedule A go on to say—

> *Describe the real estate in enough detail so that the IRS can easily locate it for inspection and valuation. For each parcel of real estate, report the* [geographic] *area and, if the parcel is improved, describe the improvements. For city or town property, report the street or number, ward subdivision, block and lot, etc. For rural property, report the township, range, landmarks, etc.*

There is a crucial point being made by the above instructions. Of all your gross estate holdings, real estate is the principal target for "inspection and valuation" by the IRS. This is because, in most cases, real estate comprises the dominant dollar value item. For practical purposes, transfer tax rates for real estate *start* at 35% to 40%. Consequently, there is temptation to low value real estate rather than fair market value it. The IRS is fully aware of this temptation. The more parcels and types of real property that a decedent has, the more professional appraisals are needed, and the more complicated his Schedule A becomes.

Schedules B & C: Intangibles

As per Figure 8.3, Schedule B (Form 706) is titled: *Stocks and Bonds*, whereas Schedule C is titled: *Mortgages, Notes, & Cash*. Both of these schedules require the listing of intangible property: "pieces of paper," as was mentioned previously. So, what is the difference between these two schedules?

The short answer is that Schedule B addresses *variable* unit-value assets, whereas Schedule C addresses *fixed*-value assets. The intangibles listed on Schedule B are more commonly known as *portfolio* assets, whereas those on Schedule C are more commonly known as *monetary* assets. Very substantial amounts of wealth can be aggregated in Schedules B and C.

Schedule B has a special column of its own, expressly headed: *Unit value*. In this column are entered such amounts as $/unit, $/share, $/contract, or $/ownership interest. Then in the description column, the number of units, shares, contracts, or ownership interests are stated. In addition to ordinary stocks and bonds, ownership interests in mutual funds, real estate investment trusts, mortgage-backed securities, limited partnerships, mining exploration activities, oil and gas wells, foreign securities, and a host of other derivative interests are listed on Schedule B.

As to the assets prescribed for Schedule C: *Mortgages, Notes, & Cash*, the instructions say—

List items on Schedule C in the following order:

- *mortgages (payable to the decedent),*
- *promissory notes (payable to the decedent),*
- *contracts to sell land,*
- *cash in possession, and*
- *cash in banks . . . and other financial organizations.*

Mortgages payable to the decedent generally arise from self-financing of real estate sales, or from monies advanced in the form of second trust deeds secured by real property. A mortgage is an enforceable instrument which has a face value, an unpaid balance, rate of interest, and date of maturity. Seller-financed mortgages are especially attractive as a simplifying endeavor where there are multiple holdings of real estate. Mortgages can be reassigned to one or more of the decedent's heirs without the appraisal, title, and management complexities of real property itself.

Cash holdings in the form of promissory notes, land contracts, savings accounts, certificates of deposit, money market funds, and checking accounts often comprise a very significant portion of a decedent's estate. The liquidity of such assets makes them the ideal focus for serious estate-simplifying effort.

Schedule D — Life Insurance

Officially, Schedule D (Form 706) is titled: *Insurance on the Decedent's Life*. Said insurance is treated as an asset of the decedent. Ordinarily, a testator does not think of insurance on his own life as being a form of property. Yet, it is. Especially, when you think of it as the "storing of money." Insurance premiums are paid in a way that, before death, each policy has a determinable cash value. At the instant of death, its cash value is substantially enhanced. It is for this reason that the headnote instruction to Schedule D says, emphatically:

*You must list **all** policies on the life of the decedent and attach a Form 712 for each policy.*

Form 712 is titled: **Life Insurance Statement**. The "statement" provides information on the face amount of the policy, amount of one sum proceeds, value of proceeds as of date of death (if not payable as one sum), name of beneficiaries, and name of the policy owner. Other instructions to Form 712 say—

If decedent is not owner, attach copy of [insurance] *application. If policy has been assigned* [to other than the decedent or his estate], *attach a copy of the assignment.*

Schedule D is the direct consequence of IRC Section 2042: *Proceeds of Life Insurance*. The gist of which is—

The value of the gross estate shall include the value of all property—

(1) Receivable by the executor . . . to the extent of the amount . . . as insurance under policies on the life of the decedent.

(2) Receivable by other beneficiaries . . . [if] *the decedent possessed at his death any of the incidents of ownership* [of the policy on his life], *exercisable either alone or in conjunction with any other person* [or entity].

To include or not include the proceeds of life insurance on Schedule D (Form 706) has been a controversy of long standing between the IRS and the insurance industry. This controversy arises because Irrevocable Life Insurance Trusts (ILITs) are marketed as being excludable from gross estates. The IRS has argued successfully that if proceeds from a life insurance trust are used to pay the estate tax, or any other taxes, debts, or charges against the decedent, such proceeds **are includible** (on Schedule D).

Schedules E & F — Other Property Items

Schedules E and F are titled, respectively: *Jointly Owned Property*, and *Other Miscellaneous Property Not Reportable Under Any Other Schedule*. Schedule E is arranged in two parts (jointly owned with spouse, and jointly owned with others), whereas Schedule F starts off with three probing Yes-No questions. Both Schedules E and F are regarded as catchalls for those assets that do not expressly qualify for inclusion on Schedules A, B, and C: real estate, stocks and bonds, and cash.

Part 1 of Schedule E: *Qualified Joint Interests Held by Decedent and Spouse* overlaps with those items in Schedules A, B, and C. The significance of Part 1 is that there is a separate one-half (or 50%) line that applies, once the marital assets are itemized and totaled. If numerous assets are so held, listing them on Schedules A, B, and C, then subtracting 50%, is more convenient than listing them in Part 1 of Schedule E.

Part 2 of Schedule E directs attention to "all other" surviving co-tenants. The form is set up for listing separately the name, address, and percentage ownership of each co-tenant. For each property so identified (and full valued), the *inclusion percentage* of the decedent is stated. Otherwise the instructions say—

If you believe that less than the full value of the entire property is includible in the gross estate for tax purposes, you must establish the right to include the smaller value by attaching proof of the extent, origin, and nature of the decedent's interest and the interest(s) of the decedent's co-tenant or co-tenants.

The headportion of Schedule F: *Other Miscellaneous Property*, directs specific attention to—

* Articles of artistic or collectible value,
* Bonus or awards to other than decedent as a result of decedent's employment or death, and
* Access to a safe deposit box.

Below the Yes-No safe deposit box question, instructions say—

If any of the contents of the safe deposit box are omitted from the schedules in this return, explain fully why omitted.

In other respects, Schedule F is a pure catchall for extraneous forms of assets which decedents and others are often unaware that they have. A listing of the types of items commonly involved is presented in Figure 8.4. The general idea behind Figure 8.4 is that nothing is to be omitted from Form 706 (if it has a value of $100 or more per item).

Schedules G, H, & I

Without question, Form 706 is THE most exhaustive tax return ever prepared for an individual. No asset can be omitted if the decedent had even the remotest of ownership interest in, or strings attached to, property which had ever been transferred during life for

Sched. F	Other Miscellaneous Property	Form 706

1. Articles of artistic or collectible value ☐ Yes ☐ No
2. Bonus or award to spouse or other ☐ Yes ☐ No
3. Access to a safe deposit box ☐ Yes ☐ No

Items Inherited or Gifted From Others

☐ Debts due decedent   ☐ Proprietorship business(es)   ☐ Insurance on life of another

● Partnership interests   ● Closely-held corporations

• Claims	• Judgments	• Farm machinery
• Refunds	• Trust funds	• Farm products
• Rights	• Automobiles	• Recreational vehicles
• Royalties	• Household goods	• Reversionary interests
• Leaseholds	• Personal effects	• Remainder interests

Fig. 8.4 - Range of Items Includible on Schedule F (706)

less than "full and adequate" consideration. This means rummaging back many years into the decedent's prior life. For this rummaging process, there are Schedules G, H, and I to be addressed. The respective titles of these schedules are—

G — *Transfers During Decedent's Life*
H — *Powers of Appointment*
I — *Annuities*

The 2,000 words of instructions to **Schedule G** start off by requiring that—

*All transfers (other than outright transfers for full and adequate consideration and bona fide sales) made by the decedent **at any time during** life must be reported on Schedule G regardless of whether you* [the Executor] *believe the transfers* [of money or property] *are subject to tax.*

This includes all transfers within three years of death, all retained life estates, all retained voting rights, all reversionary interests, all revocable transfers, and all transfers taking effect at death.

The 900 words of instructions to **Schedule H** start off by requiring that—

Include in the gross estate: (1) The value of the property for which the decedent possessed a general power of appointment on his or her death; and (2) The value of property for which [the decedent] *exercised or released the power before death by disposing of it in such a way that it would* [otherwise be treated] *... as a retained life estate, a transfer taking effect at death, or a revocable transfer.*

A "power of appointment" is the right of a decedent to enjoy all or part of the property of someone else which is in trust, under contract, or sequestered by insurance or other arrangement. A power is not includible in the gross estate if the decedent released the power completely and the decedent held no interest in or control over the property.

The 3,000 words of instructions to **Schedule I** start off by requiring that—

Include in the gross estate the value of any annuity that: (1) Is receivable by a beneficiary following the death of a decedent by reason of surviving the decedent; or (2) Is payable to the decedent ... for life ... or for any period that did not in fact end before the decedent's death.

An "annuity" is a contract for payments over a period of time referenced to the decedent's life. Includibility depends on who purchased the contract: the decedent, his employer, or someone else. Whatever portion the decedent purchased is always includible.

It should be obvious by now that very little property of value, or rights to the enjoyment of such property, escapes the corralling arm of Form 706. No matter what you have accumulated or have tried to preserve during life, it is **all** resurrected at time of death. After subtractions for debts, expenses, fees, and taxes, that which remains is available for distribution to heirs and beneficiaries ... either by will or by trust.

9

IDENTIFYING DISTRIBUTEES

A Declarant (Testator/Trustor) Demonstrates Soundness Of Mind By Adequately Identifying His Intended Recipients (Distributees) Of Money And Property When He Dies. Whether Doing So In A Will Or In A Trust, One's Family Status Must Be Cited With Specificity And Clarity. Family Members Comprise One's "Natural Heirs" Should Ambiguities Arise Re One's Status Of Marriage, Divorce, Remarriage, Or Widowhood. For Wealthy Declarants Whose Children Also Are Well Off, Generation-Skipping Transfers Are Attractive. Current Distributees Are Those Prescribed By Will; Future Distributees Are Prescribed By Trust.

The term *distributee* refers to each separate recipient of money or property from a decedent. A distributee may be an heir, a beneficiary, or other person. An "heir" is a person who would inherit the decedent's property under the laws of intestate succession, if no will or trust were in effect. Otherwise, an heir is a direct descendant of the decedent, namely: his children and grandchildren, on down the line. A "beneficiary" is a direct family member of the decedent, such as his surviving spouse, brother, sister, parent, and grandparent. An "other person" is a relative, close friend, or other person or entity who has been helpful to the decedent when he was alive. All are "distributees" for testamentary purposes.

It is important that each intended distributee be identified with clarity and specificity. Included in this clarity feature are the type and amount of the decedent's property intended to be distributed. It should be noted, though, that no money or property should be distributed until all affairs of the decedent's estate have been settled. This means that all applicable taxes, debts, expenses of administration, and professional fees should be addressed before the first distributee receives his or her dollars or dollars' worth of property. Exceptions are granted where there is clear evidence of early (partial) need.

The best reason for distributee clarity and his/her property share specificity is the avoidance of — or at least the minimization of — probate proceedings. All litigative stances threatening probate can be costly and time consuming. They can seriously diminish the net distributable assets of a decedent. Why more distributees are not aware of this diminution aspect of probate litigation is always puzzling to executors and trustees.

Accordingly, in this chapter we want to describe those features which are desirable for enhancing the clarity of a decedent's intent. For this, we want to explain the importance of stating up front one's family status. One's "family" comprises his/her rightful heirs should ambiguities of interpretation arise. If a declarant has no family — that is, neither children nor siblings — he/she is vulnerable to "death bed switching" of asset intentions. We present a true life example that will open your eyes to such dangers. We also offer a few words on generation-skipping transfers which are attractive to wealthy testators/trustors.

Cite Family Status First

Whether it is a will or a trust that is under interpretation, the full names and relationships of all direct-line family members should be identified. This should be done within the first few paragraphs of the testamentary instrument. By so doing, the presumption is that, unless subsequent contrary statements are made, the family members are those who will ultimately receive the lion's share of the decedent's estate. For this reason, the precise spelling of names and the correct family relationship must be stated. Each testator/trustor makes the statement in the form of a declaration.

A typical such "family first" declaration might read something like this [all names are strictly fictitious]:

I, JOHN QUINCY JONES, hereby declare that I am married to MARY JANE (MORGAN) JONES, and that we have three children, namely: a son, DAVID MARK JONES, age approximately 30 years; a daughter, JANE ELIZABETH JONES, age approximately 20 years, and a son, JOSEPH SCOTT JONES, age approximately 10 years.

Correct full names are important to avoid mis-identities of persons with similar names. In the case of a married woman, citing her maiden name in parentheses (as shown above) can be helpful when tracing any separate property acquired by gift or inheritance from her parents. Identifying the relationship to the testator also helps avoid mis-identities. Giving approximate ages helps to distinguish between adults and minors. If the age of a minor child becomes a critical matter in estate distribution(s), that child's birth certificate can always be produced later.

Applying our clarity standard, do you have any difficulty knowing who the above-named persons are, and their relationships to the declarant? Even if there are other persons named subsequently whose name(s) and relationship(s) are not crystal clear, the testator/trustor has displayed adequate capacity of mind. He later cannot be faulted for fuzzy intentions with respect to distributee identifications.

Note that we have capitalized each prospective distributee's name. This makes a name easier to find when flipping back from many pages later, where specific distributions are indicated. In most cases, the property distributions are identified by using (capitalized) first names only. This one feature alone greatly simplifies distributive intent.

Clarifying Other Names

We have cited above, intentionally, a simple set of names. Each is identified by first name, by a middle name, and by a last name. This is a rather conventional way in "ordinary" U.S. family culture. Other cultures have different naming practices. There may be two first names, two middle names, and/or two last names. Each must be spelled out in full, at least in the initial family description declaration.

In U.S. business practice — including one's name on a U.S. tax return — rarely is a middle name used in full. An initial is used instead. In testamentary documentation, the use of an initial alone can cause identity confusion. Take the case of DAVID MARK JONES, the 30-year-old son above. Say the father cites his name as **David M. Jones**. For reasons not relevant here, David prefers to be called: **Mark D. Jones**. All of his business papers refer to him as Mark D. rather than David M. When the father dies and bequests $1,000,000 or so to David M. Jones, for example, can't you sense the litigative posturing when trying to prove that David M. Jones and Mark D. Jones are one and the same? Wouldn't it be easier to prove "one and the same" if the transposed names were David Mark Jones or Mark David Jones, absent any middle initial only?

Adult children tend to interchange first and middle names as they see fit. When they do, the **a.k.a.** (also known as) is testator/trustor prudent. Always start with a birth given full name first, than switch it around as per the distributee's preference or business practice:

DAVID MARK JONES, a.k.a. DAVID M. JONES, a.k.a. MARK DAVID JONES, a.k.a. MARK D. JONES.

Yes, of course, the birth name of an adult child can be officially changed by a court order. Should this take place, it is still prudent to cite the birth given name followed by the court-ordered change. A certified copy of the court-ordered change should be attached to the testamentary instrument, be it a will or a trust. Such an attachment is particularly advised when a large distributive share of the decedent's estate is contemplated.

If there is no birth certificate given or court-ordered middle name or middle initial, so indicate in parentheses with the letters **n.m.n.** (no middle name) or **n.m.i.** (no middle initial). Example: DAVID (n.m.n.) JONES or DAVID (n.m.i.) JONES. This invalidates any middle name or middle initial that might be voluntarily taken on by the distributee unbeknown to the testator/trustor. If DAVID has two middle names or two middle initials, state them.

In the case of a married daughter, show the testator's family name in parentheses, followed by her married name. Example; JANE ELIZABETH (JONES) SMITH. This clarifies immediately Jane's relationship to her father, whose family name is JONES. If Jane had been working before her marriage and had established a professional identity of her own, a hyphenated double last name can be used to convey the same relationship. Example: JANE ELIZABETH JONES-SMITH. Working young women often prefer this arrangement until their first or second child is beyond the toddler stage. If no children, and divorce ensues, the married name SMITH can be dropped, and the maiden name JONES can be resumed.

Deceased Married Child

One concern that often arises when identifying distributees pertains to one or more married children of the testator. The spouses of married children are strangers in blood to the testamentary declarant. They are not his natural heirs. If he wishes to make provision for them, he can. But he cannot be faulted if no provisions are made. Especially so, if the parents of the child's spouse intend to make distributee provisions for their own child who is now married.

The distributee situation changes markedly when one of the married children of the testator dies. If the deceased married child had no issue (that is, no grandchildren for the testator), the deceased child's inheritance could go one of two ways. It could be redistributed to the testator's other children. Or, it could be directed to the estate of the deceased married child. If this latter option were used, the deceased child's spouse would become the beneficial distributee. This certainly would be the right thing to do, if the deceased child were a son and his widowed wife were pregnant with another child of the son.

To expand the declaratory intentions above, let us assume that David is married and has two children of his own (Thomas and Kate). Further assume that David is deceased at the time John (the testator) prepares his will. The heirs that should be declared in John's will are depicted in Figure 9.1. Note in Figure 9.1 that David's spouse (a blood stranger to John) is omitted. By naming David's two children (John's grandchildren), David's spouse has no valid claim to John's estate. If, on the other hand, David's children are not named, David's spouse could petition the court for David's share of John's estate. The court would have to honor the petition, if David had a will leaving everything to David's wife.

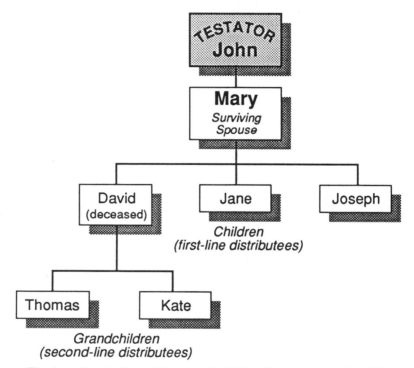

Fig. 9.1 - Illustration of Descendant Distributees to be Identified

When a predeceased child has children (as in Figure 9.1) and the testator intends to make distribution to them (his grandchildren), they should be clearly named as substitutes for the deceased child. To illustrate one way of declaring so, John's will could read as—

I, JOHN QUINCY JONES, hereby declare that I am married to MARY JANE (MORGAN) JONES, and that we have three children, namely: DAVID MARK JONES, now deceased; a daughter, JANE ELIZABETH JONES, age approximately 20 years; and a son, JOSEPH SCOTT JONES, age approximately 10 years. My deceased son DAVID is survived by THOMAS QUINCY JONES, age approximately 8 years, and KATE DOROTHY JONES, age approximately 6 years, for both of whom I intend to make provision herein.

Assume for the moment that David's wife was named Patricia. Her name is not shown on Figure 9.1 as she is a blood stranger to John. However, if David's two children were minors when John deceased, Patricia would be the natural guardian of David's children and of their inheritance from John. As the grandparent, John would have no choice in this matter.

Divorce and Remarriage

Another situation that occurs often these days involves divorce and remarriage. It is estimated that nearly 50% of all marriages between ages 20 and 30 end in divorce. If this happens, careful blood-relation distinctions must be made when the testator declares his/her heirs. Upon divorce (final), the ex-spouse becomes a stranger for inheritance purposes.

In the above declaration, suppose that John had been married previously and was divorced before marrying Mary. Suppose, too, that Mary had been married previously and was divorced before marrying John. Suppose further that John had two children by his previous marriage; Mary had two children by her previous marriage; and between them John and Mary had two children of their own. Thus, six children are involved (none of whom are grandchildren).

Since John and Mary are separate testators, each will have different first-line heirs (distributees). Each will have four heirs, of which two will be in common with each other, and two not. That is, John's two children by his former marriage, while his blood heirs, will be strangers in blood to Mary. Similarly, Mary's two children by her former marriage, while her direct heirs, will be strangers to John. This situation is depicted in Figure 9.2. John's ex-spouse is a

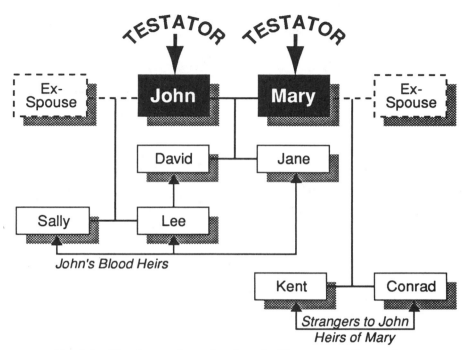

Fig. 9.2 - Distributee Complications in Divorce and Remarriage

stranger, so there's no need to name her in his will as a distributee. However, the fact of the divorce should be made clear. John's four heirs are Sally (age 20), Lee (age 18), David (age 15), and Jane (age 5). Mary's four heirs are Kent (age 19), Conrad (age 17), David (age 15), and Jane (age 5).

In declaratory form, then, John's testamentary declaration might read—

> *I, JOHN QUINCY JONES, hereby declare that I am married to MARY JANE (MORGAN) (WHITE) JONES, and that we have two children by this marriage, namely: DAVID MARK JONES, age approximately 15 years and JANE ELIZABETH JONES, age approximately 5 years. In addition, I have two children by a previous marriage, namely: SALLY ANN JONES, age approximately 20 years, and LEE MORRIS JONES, age approximately 18 years. I was previously married*

to MARGARET ANN (MOOREHEAD) JONES and we divorced on March 10, 1993.

John has no obligation to name Mary's children by her previous marriage in his will. They are not his blood heirs. However, if John were to legally adopt Mary's two children, then they would be his distributees. Adopted children take on the same lineal heritage as the parents who adopt them.

In a divorce and remarriage situation, legal challenges to a testamentary instrument upon death are highly likely. This would be particularly true where an ex-spouse were the legal custodian of the decedent testator/trustor's minor children. Ex-spousal effort, rightly so, would be made to assure that a remarried decedent parent had provided adequately for his/her children. Here's a situation where it would be prudent to have the divorce decree readily accessible for reference. Unfortunately, as remarital time goes on, divorce decrees and other related legal papers tend to get lost or misplaced, in the hustle and bustle of family living.

5 Classes of Children

Except for wealth and divorce, and possibly other special circumstances, rarely does a married couple with children bequeath property directly to their children. Instead, each parent bequeaths to the surviving parent, who in turn bequeaths to the surviving children. This assumes, of course, that the surviving parent does not remarry.

Contrary to first thoughts by testating parents, all children in a family need not be identified in general terms (as we've done above) that imply that all children share equally in the parental property. The post-parent needs of each child will differ. Much depends on age, general health (such as disabled), education level and aspirations, whether or not married (with children of their own), nature of employment, general economic level, and degree of financial maturity. Rarely are two children of the same parents exactly alike as to their property needs and financial acumen.

As we see it, there are five classes of children for testamentary consideration. These are—

1. *Mature adults*:	mid-thirties in age who can handle money responsibly
2. *Young adults*:	ages 20 to 35 with voracious spending appetites
3. *Spendthrifts*:	of legal age who are drifters in life, mostly unemployed, and without goals
4. *Minors & disabled*:	having special needs and requiring the appointment of guardian(s)
5. *Children of divorce*:	any age; complicated by parental loyalty; bequests on "case by case" basis

We summarize the identification situation for you in Figure 9.3. In all cases, there has to be some type of predeceasement clause that makes it clear that, should a child not survive the parent, that child's issue, if any, shall "step into" that deceased child's shoes.

The easiest class of children to provide for is those who are adults . . . and financially mature. These are children who are "thirty-something" in age. This is the age beyond which persons of ordinary intelligence and responsibility can handle money and property prudently. While they can still make mistakes with money, they are not prone to blowing it foolishly and lavishly. Typically, this age is 35 and over.

Recognizing some age of financial maturity is important for testamentary purposes It means that a testator can bequeath his estate outright to one or more such children and be done with it. He need not set up an elaborate trust scheme to distribute his estate annually in prescribed increments. Each financially mature child receives his or her prorata share of the testator's estate. Thereafter, each such child is on his or her own.

As to the other classes of children signified in Figure 9.3, we address them more directly in Chapter 12: Writing Your Own Will. Identifying them is more than just citing their names and ages alone. Some more descriptive characteristic has to be added to convey parental concern and reason or nonequal and non-immediate property distribution. These are case-by-case family matters.

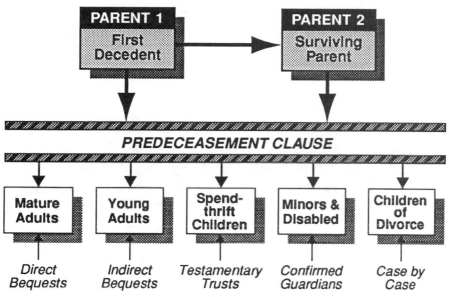

Fig. 9.3 - "Classes" of Children for Testamentary Identifications

Married Without Children

When a couple is married and has no children, a different testamentary perspective looms. If natural or adopted children are not on the horizon, who does each spouse identify as his/her distributee? Does the first decedent spouse leave it all to the surviving spouse who, in turn, identifies separately his or her choice of distributees? Or, does each spouse identify his/her own distributees with the "understanding" that each set of distributees is honored fully when the surviving spouse dies? To accommodate any such understanding, a trust instrument in one form or another (living, testamentary, or irrevocable) is clearly advisable.

A living trust, also known as an *inter vivos* trust (between the living) is covered by the thrust of this book. It is created before either spousal death. A testamentary trust, on the other hand, is created **at** time of death, as expressed in each spouse's will. An irrevocable trust is created before death by the irrevocable conveyance of money, property, gift tax return, life insurance, annuity contract, or other binding agreement. For our purposes at this point, a testamentary trust with a life estate grant to the surviving spouse would be preferred. There are no children (descendants) for which to provide for an ongoing period of time.

With the above in mind, each spousal declaratory identification of distributees might read—

> *I, JOHN QUINCY JONES, hereby declare that I am married to MARY JANE (MORGAN) JONES, and that we have no children, either natural, adopted, or deceased. I have not been married previously. I have one living parent, my mother, DOROTHY DIANE JONES; one brother, DONALD JARED JONES; and one sister, JULIE ANN (JONES) SMITH, for all of whom I intend to make provision for herein. I have no other brothers or sisters.*

As for Mary, her declaratory identification of distributees might read—

> *I, MARY JANE (MORGAN) JONES, hereby declare that I am married to JOHN QUINCY JONES, and that we have no children, either natural, adopted, or deceased. I was married previously to TIMOTHY RUSSELL BROWN, but was divorced on July 30, 2001. I have no children with TIMOTHY. Both of my parents are living, namely: my father, GEORGE JEFFERSON MORGAN, and my mother, GERALDINE DOROTHY MORGAN. I have no brothers or sisters, but I do have one adult niece, VICKIE ANGELA (MORGAN) TRUEBLOOD. I intend to make provision herein for my parents and my niece, who is married with children of her own.*

As you can sense from the identifying efforts above, when there are no children, each spouse turns first to his or her own parents. This is a form of deference and obligation to provide financial assistance to one's aging parents. Next, each spouse turns to his/her own brothers or sisters, and/or to his or her own nephews and nieces. The idea is to identify at least one of these persons who has children of his or her own. Every testator/trustor's objective is to preferably pass money and property down the family line . . . somewhere.

The moment one family member is identified, there is temptation to acknowledge all others to avoid any "hurt feelings". As a practical matter, we suggest that no attempt be made to do so. Select the one or two relatives who have minor children, and let it go at that. When there are minor children, there is always a need for inherited money.

Unmarried: No Children, No Siblings

The most risky distributee-naming situation occurs when the declarant is unmarried, has no children, no siblings, and no nephews or nieces. Here, the term "unmarried" characterizes one as either being a divorced person or a widow/widower. In contrast, one who has never been married is characterized as being single. We say that the distributee-naming process is "risky" because those whose names are cited — not being identifiable family members — can be abrogated by covetous outsiders.

If there are no natural heirs, what does a declarant do? Most commonly, he/she names his/her closest friends and favored charities. Sometimes, a declarant can get carried away in the process. He/she may identify anywhere from 10 to 25 persons, and from 5 to 15 charities, depending on the dollar magnitude of the estate to be distributed. With so many persons and so many charities involved, disputes inevitably will arise. When so many disputes arise, attorneys spring out of the woodwork from every direction. The decedent's executor becomes overwhelmed. Chaos often results.

To minimize chaotic conditions when an unmarried-no-heirs declarant dies, strong language has to be used. For illustration purposes only, our previously fictitious John Quincy Jones is now a widower without any natural heirs or beneficiaries (children, siblings, etc.). His declaration of designatee intent might read something like this—

I, JOHN QUINCY JONES, declare that I am a widower and that I was previously married to MARY JANE (MORGAN) JONES who deceased on __(date)__ . We have no children and neither MARY nor I has any siblings. In lieu thereof, I designate the following friends and charities to receive that portion of my estate prescribed separately below, to wit:

1.	*SANDRA SUSAN COLLINS*	*(address)*
2.	*NAME #2*	"
3.	*NAME #3*	"
4.	*NAME #4*	"
5.	*NAME #5*	"
•	*etc.*	"
13.	*ANIMAL RESCUE MISSION*	"
14.	*Charity #2*	"
15.	*Charity #3*	"
•	*etc.*	"

If any person named above, other than SANDRA, is deceased at the time of my demise, or who cannot be located within six months of my demise, or who engages legal counsel to contest the distributions prescribed below, said person(s) or his/her estate(s) shall be denied any participation in my estate. These same conditions apply to any of the above-listed charities. All denied participations shall accrue to the sole benefit of my close and dear friend of many years, namely: SANDRA COLLINS.

Mindful that Sandra is the catchall distributee for the loose ends of John's estate, her name should be the No. 1 listing above. Should Sandra be deceased at time of John's death, Sandra's estate would become the distributee recipient.

It would appear from the example wording above that John's distributee intentions are reasonably clear. Yes, some ambiguities of interpretation could arise after his demise. If so, the discretionary powers granted to John's executor or trustee are there to work things out should the necessity arise.

Precautions with Charities

Note the listing of charities in John's last bequests above. For a solo testator/trustor (as in John's case), one or more reputable charities constitute his or her distributees of last resort. With no close family kin to give to, giving to charity is an appealing substitute. The money and property given are used, ostensibly for good and humane causes. These causes are religiously and emotionally charged to tug at the very heart strings of every solo donor. The donated money and property are supposed to be dispensed with great kindness and service to mankind, animal kind, and plant kind. We're not so sure about this. A healthy skepticism should prevail . . . because charities are **tax exempt**.

As per IRC Section 501: *Exemption from Tax on Corporations, Certain Trusts, Etc.*, a charitable entity pays no tax of any kind. This means that such an entity can receive thousands, millions, hundreds of millions — even billions — of dollars . . . and pay no tax on it! This one fact alone often leads to abuses and misuses of bequests intended for noble causes. High salaries to officers and directors, lavish lifestyles of employees, and the corruption of accounting practices can absorb the greater portion of the revenue intake. So, when distributing a solo donor's estate money to charity, we suggest certain precautions.

All qualified charities are required to file annually with the IRS **Form 990**: *Return of Organization Exempt from Income Tax*. On this form, the correct full name of the organization, its Tax ID, its exempt type, and monetary accounting items (re revenue and expenses) are reported. There are some 27 types of 501(c) charitable organizations.

Thus, when designating a charity as a distributee of one's estate, the following information should be sought:

☐ Tax exempt name
☐ Tax ID
☐ 501(c) type (Type "3" is the most common: Religious, Educational, Charitable, etc.)

One might also request the ratio of compensation paid to officers, directors, and employees to the total revenue reported on line 12 of Form 990. One would not get this information, but it would be interesting to ask for it nevertheless. If the officer, etc. compensation ratio is 35% or higher, the charity is NOT fulfilling its exempt purpose. That charity should be avoided.

Abuse of Charity Example

We want to give you a true life example of how the charitable bequests of a solo testator can be "death bed" mishandled. It was all done in the name of the church which the decedent had attended for many years.

The testator was an 84-year-old widow, with no children and no siblings. Her predeceased husband, a small-business owner, left her financially well off. In addition to her home, her "widow's estate" consisted of roughly $2,285,000 in 22 stock holdings, five limited partnerships, and five separate bank accounts. After her husband's estate was settled, she rewrote her will. She listed 25 close friends and one distant cousin as distributees of 50% of her estate; the other 50% would go to the Welfare Fund of her local church for needy ministers and missionaries.

One of the members of her church was a female stock broker, a person some 30 years younger than the testator. The female stock broker became the testator's financial confidant and investment manager. The confidant urged the testator to sell her home and move into a newly constructed church-sponsored retirement facility.

Shortly after moving into the church retirement facility, the testator had a stroke. This left her having difficulty walking and talking. She was bedridden and hospitalized intermittently. The financial confidant learned of the testator's deteriorating physical and mental condition, and immediately contacted the church's attorney (also a female). Together, the two counselors had the testator revoke her will and authorize the creation of a Charitable Remainder Unitrust. By this time, the testator could hardly see, hear, or write. Yet, she authorized — by the nod of her head or a grunt — the creation of a trust which shut out all 25 of her will-designated lifelong friends.

Simultaneously, with preparation of the 32-page trust instrument, the testator (evidently) authorized her financial confidant to liquidate all assets excepting specific stocks. The liquidation proceeds were used to purchase additional shares of the same six stocks. Altogether, the testator, while barely alive, held 8,200 shares of oil company and utility stocks. All 8,200 shares were listed properly on "Exhibit A" of the trust instrument. The instrument provided that all shares, representing about $3,300,000 (3.3 million) were to be sold over a 6-year period and distributed to the church. The testator X-marked her signature. The X-mark was attested to by the church attorney and the stock broker. A separate attorney (also a female) prepared the trust instrument. About five days later, the testator died.

This is the classic case of what is known as the *death-bed switch*! The church attorney and the stock broker took over. There was no death tax accounting because all assets were charitably donated; there was no probate because the trust was legally executed before death; there was no communication of any kind to the 25 testator-designated distributees. The quiet rearrangement into a stock portfolio in the name of the church trust generated an estimated $186,000 PER YEAR in commissions for the stock broker. The rearrangement also generated for the church attorney approximately $150,000 PER YEAR in legal fees. Over the 6-year trust administration period, the commissions, fees, and other expenses totaled nearly $2,300,000. The church got the remainder: approximately $1,000,000. Now you know why we urge caution when solo bequeathing to charity.

Generation-Skipping Transfers

As you can sense from all of that which has been previously presented, identifying distributees and providing for them becomes more ambiguous as a family unit ages. Particularly so, when one or more children are married, divorced, remarried, deceased, and have children of their own. Once grandchildren come on the scene, a family trust begins to appear more attractive than does an ordinary will. A will, however is still a prerequisite to a trust in that it enables the *other living* potential distributees to be identified.

For wealthy families, whose children themselves are well off, the idea of a generation-skipping trust is appealing Though appealing, it is complicated. It is so, because the trustors have to identify not only persons "then living," but also persons *yet unborn*. The only practical way to identify yet unborns is to describe them through generational assignments. To get a quick handle on how generational assignments are made, you need to know the definition of a "skip person."

IRC Section 2613(a) defines a skip person as—

(1) *a natural person assigned to a generation which is 2 or more generations below the generation assignment of the transferor, OR*

(2) *a trust . . . if all* [property] *interests in such trust are held by skip persons . . . and at no time after such transfer* [into trust] *may a distribution . . . be made from such trust to a non-skip person.*

Another way of saying this is that a skip person is a grandchild (2nd generational line), a great grandchild (3rd generational line), and a great great grandchild (4th generational line). The transferor is the parent who "skips over" his own children, including those family members across his children's generational assignment. Contrary to ordinary logic, a skipped-over person is tax defined as a non-skip person. The term "non-skip" derives from the fact that said person is NOT a distributee of the transferor's **property**.

For an arrangement to qualify as a GST (Generation Skipping Transfer) trust, the property/corpus transfers from the trustor/transferor must ultimately go to all skip persons. Non-skip persons may be included in the trust instrument, but only to the extent that they are *income* recipients: not corpus recipients. It is important, therefore, that the GST trust instrument make the distinction clear as to which beneficiaries are skip persons and which are non-skip persons.

Under ordinary familial conditions, a GST trust would provide for non-skip persons as well as for its skip persons. Because non-skip persons receive no corpus from the trust, they get priority on all of its income. A non-skip person may disclaim all of his/her income share or may decline part of it. In such case, the disclaimed/declined income would go to other non-skip persons (or to skip persons) having the most financial need.

A *generation assignment* references the date of birth of the transferor and uses a 25-year band ($12^1/2$ years before and $12^1/2$

years after) for establishing a new generation every 25 years. Such is our portrayal in Figure 9.4.

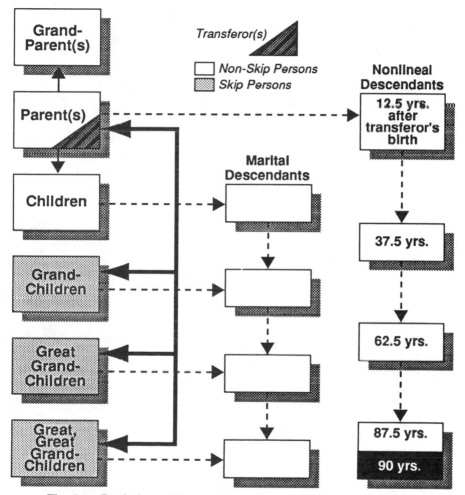

Fig. 9.4 - Depiction of Generational Groupings for GST Purposes

Once a generation-skipping arrangement is established and its techniques mastered, the familial desire is to go on and on, ad infinitum. Perpetual family trusts are envisioned for transferring property interests down generational lines to unnamed and yet-to-be-born distributees. Such a goal contradicts the common-law rule against perpetuities. The premise of common law is that, if a property interest conveyed by trust does not vest in some life-in-being within 21 years after the death of an individual alive at the time the trust was created, the interest is invalid.

In no event, however, shall a distributee's interest extend more than 90 years after the GST arrangement was created. We had this anti-perpetuity rule in mind when we displayed in Figure 9.4 the dark bold box labeled "90 yrs" at the very end of the third column. Overall, therefore, we see no validity in a GST trust conveying property interests to more than three generations of skip persons.

The whole idea of identifying the distributees of a decedent's property is to earmark that property for distributing it all! There are three ways for doing this. One is by will; the second is by an ordinary trust; the third is by a GST trust. Those persons designated to receive property by will are called: *current distributees*. Those designated by trust are called: future distributees or, more commonly, *trust beneficiaries*. When a will directs the dominant portion of a decedent's property into a trust — be it an ordinary or GST trust — the trust entity itself becomes a current distributee.

10

THE PROBATE PROCESS

The Term "Probate" Often Has A Bad Reputation. Cronyism Of The Legal System Where The Decedent Last Resided Is Largely To Blame. Even So, The Process Has Distinct Virtues. Foremost Is That It Assures Creditors, Critics, Beneficiaries, And Others That "Things Were Done Right." If A Nonattorney, The Will-Appointed Executor Can Do Whatever Is Necessary With Legal LETTERS TESTAMENTARY. Preprinted Check-The-Box Probate Forms Are Available As An Aid In Populous States. Notice Of Death Must Be Published Inviting All "Financially Interested" Persons To Appear At A COURT HEARING.

Probate. You've heard the term. It's something that executors and distributees hate. Attorneys and the legal system love it. Testators fear it; trustors think they have bypassed it. More than any one single factor, the fear of probate has caused many testators to pay attorneys to prepare a living trust which, for modest estates, is quite unnecessary. For gross estates in the up-to-$1,000,000-plus range, joint tenancy with right of survivorship would serve just as well as a living trust.

Having stated the above, it is still important that a property owner (testator/trustor) and his appointed personal representative at time of death (executor/trustee) know something about the probate process. A little pre-knowledge on the subject can go a long way towards reducing the fear and trepidation of probating a will or of probating an ambiguous statement or clause in a trust. A little pre-knowledge will also help an executor or trustee fend off intimidating probes by covetous and unscrupulous attorneys.

Except in very rare cases, the probate process is quite perfunctory. Certain preprinted forms have to be filed. Certain public notices have to be given. And certain accounting statements have to be made. There is no jury trial. The court clerk does most of the key elements of paper processing; the presiding judge does most of the questioning and more often than not renders his decision from the bench.

Accordingly, in this chapter we want to tone down the fear and uncertainty associated with probate and discuss the process in matter-of-fact terms. We want to do this in a way that, if an executor or trustee had to, he could initiate the process on his own. Legal counsel is needed only in the most contentious of cases. Where obstructionist heirs and beneficiaries are making harassing and unreasonable demands, and their attorneys are threatening to have an executor or trustee removed, probate may be the only way to get hostile adversaries off of one's back. For this reason, we feel that conscientious executors and trustees must know the rudiments of the probate process for their own self protection.

The Purpose of Probate

Putting all fears aside, there is a fundamental reason for the probate process. It is to give public notice that a certain person has died and that his/her last will is available for examination. In the published notice, an opportunity is offered to financially interested parties to come forth and state their claims, if any, against the decedent's estate. At the same time, objections, if any, may be lodged with the probate court concerning the appointment and capability of the will-named executor. The whole idea is to "clear the air" concerning a decedent's estate so that his/her property can pass to designated distributees without subsequent legal challenge.

The probate process is a *state law* affair; it is NOT a federal law matter whatsoever. Jurisdiction rests with the superior court of the state and county where the decedent legally resided at time of death. One's "legal residence" — often called: *domicile* — is an individual's permanent home or principal establishment to which he or she intends to return for prolonged periods. Once a decedent's state of legal residence is established, that state's Probate Code becomes the official guide for conducting the probate process.

As we've done in previous chapters, we cite from the California Probate Code (CPC) to illustrate certain points. For starters, we cite CPC § 7001: *Administration of decedent's property*—

The decedent's property is subject to administration under this code, except as otherwise provided by law, and is subject to the rights of beneficiaries, creditors, and other persons as provided by law.

Note that the focus is on the decedent's **property** and on those who have *rights* to it. There are three classes of rights persons, namely: creditors, others, and beneficiaries. Creditors have priority rights to a decedent's property. This is because, before his or her death, legal commitments were made to repay all valid creditors in full. Second in line are "other persons." These are those who inventory, appraise, manage, and protect the property during its period of administration. Other person claims are for professional fees, funeral expenses, administrative costs, legal costs (if any), and taxes assessed after death.

The term "administration" constitutes the probate process itself. Administration is a form of judicial oversight until such time as the decedent's property is ready to pass to those persons (beneficiaries/distributees) expressly designated in the decedent's will. As per CPC § 12200: *Petition for final distribution order*, the executor must close the estate within 12 months after being issued Letters Testamentary (if no federal Form 706 is required) or within 18 months (if such federal form is required). The overall scheme of the process is portrayed in Figure 10.1. As should be evident in this figure, the process focuses primarily on a decedent's *will* rather than on his or her trust.

Pre-Visit the Probate Court

There is one "best way" for a nonattorney to get a realistic handle on the probate process. Actually go visit the probate court on

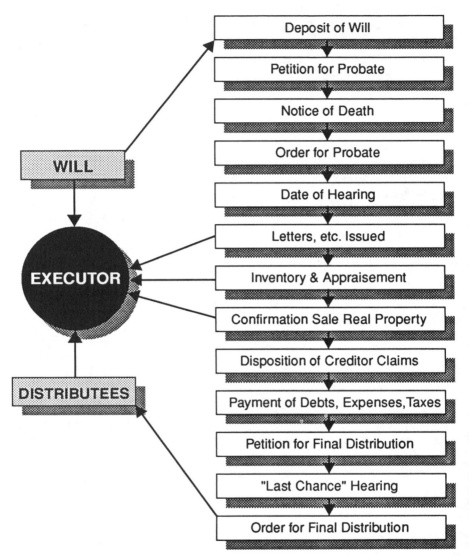

Fig. 10.1 - General Sequence of Key Probative Events

one's own. Said court is usually (but not always) located in the largest city of the *county* where the decedent was domiciled. If not the largest city, it is "county seat" regardless of population size. Its specific address and location can be found in a telephone directory or from the internet. A phone call or an internet search can provide its hours of operation. You do not have to be a petitioner or respondent to go into the courtroom, sit in the back, and observe the goings on. Go early in the morning when the court first opens and the "calendar calls" are made. Matters move quickly from this point in time on.

Before stepping inside the courtroom door, look for the file of cases-to-be-called posted nearby. Make a few hand notes of some of the case numbers and petitioner names. Then walk in the door, take a seat, and be quiet. You want to observe first-hand the perfunctoriness of the proceedings.

After the presiding judge takes his seat at the bench, he instructs the court clerk to call the first case. The clerk reads off the case number, the name of the decedent, and the type of petition, then hands that case file to the judge. The judge reads the petitioner's name and asks if he is present. (He'd better be present!)

To which the petitioner responds: "Present, your honor." The judge then asks: "Any objections?" or other appropriate query. If no response, the judge scribbles his signature on the appropriate approval form and hands the file back to the clerk. The judge then utters: "Next case."

If there is any objection to the petition for papers or authority being sought, the objector and petitioner are sworn in by the clerk. The judge permits each side to state a position, makes a few inquiries of his own, then, in most cases, renders a decision on the spot. The clerk notes the decision on the filed papers, then invites the petitioner and objector to meet in his office after the calendar is completed.

If there was a petitioner who is a nonattorney, follow that person out when he or she leaves the courtroom. Introduce yourself, then make a few inquiries indicating your eagerness to learn more about the process without an attorney. Ask for any suggestions or pointers that might be helpful to you. Particularly ask that petitioner where he or she was able to purchase *preprinted* probate forms.

In California, for example, preprinted probate forms are prepared by various state bar association members and submitted to a Judicial Council for approval. After approval, the forms are made available for statewide use. California has some 35 preprinted probate forms. Often they are available for inspection or for photocopying at the county law library (usually in the vicinity of the probate court). County law libraries are tax-exempt entities and, therefore, are usable by all taxpayers. Go there and ask the librarian about them and where you may purchase them.

Check-the-Box Type Forms

There are two especially nice features about the California preprinted probate forms. One, all of the legal terminology and phrases applicable to the title of the form are preprinted directly thereon. This materially reduces the chance of error and thereby reduces the number of rejections when submitting a form to the probate clerk for filing.

The second great feature is that each preprinted form is loaded with checkboxes. You simply check the box that applies. Use either a √-mark or an X-mark. Those that do not apply, leave blank. Yes, there are a few blank spaces where you have to make hand entries, such as: name of decedent, name of petitioner, name of probate court, etc. In addition, certain attachments are required and are so stated on the form. Otherwise, the probate documents are conspicuously check-the-box type forms.

To illustrate the practicality of check-the-box forms, we use California form **DE-111**: *Petition for Probate*. Overall, this form displays about 75 checkboxes, unequally among eight separate items. Keep in mind that this and other probate forms are designed to accommodate a broad range of decedents' estate matters and distributees. Common sense tells you that you do not check all boxes. All displayed boxes could not possibly apply simultaneously to one decedent's estate.

As an example of what we mean, we abbreviate, in Figure 10.2, *Item 2* of form DE-111 [the "DE" is Decedent's Estate]. Of the 12 checkboxes there, how many boxes would you √- or X-mark?

Before you can answer, we need to give you certain information. A common situation is that of a close family member being appointed as executor in the decedent's will. Accompanying this appointment are statements to the effect that no bond is required and that the executor shall perform his duties without supervision of the court. The phrase "without supervision of the court" refers to the

---

| HEADING FORMAT

☐ **Petition for Probate** | *For Court
Use Only* |

X X X X X X X X X X X X X X X X X X X X X X X X X X X X X X X X

2. Petitioner requests that -

a. ☐ decedent's will be admitted to probate

b. ☐ _____ be appointed as

    (1) ☐ executor   (3) ☐ administrator

    (2) ☐ administrator with   (4) ☐ special administrator
          will annexed

c. ☐ authority be granted (for) **Independent Administration**

    (1) ☐ **with** full authority to act

    (2) ☐ **without** authority (re) sale of real property

d. ☐ bond not be required

    (1) ☐ $ _____ bond be fixed

    (2) ☐ $ _____ in blocked account be allowed
             (as alternative to bond)

X X X X X X X X X X X X X X X X X X X X X X X X X X X X X X X X

Fig. 10.2 - Example of Check-the-Box Options Preprinted on Probate Form

provisions of *The Independent Administration of Estates Act.* We'll comment more on this Act later.

Now, back to Figure 10.2. Based on the information just given to you, how many of the 12 boxes would you check?

Answer: Six, namely: box a, box b, box b(1), box c, box c(1), and box d.

Note in Figure 10.2 that box c has two subboxes: (1) *with full authority* and (2) *without authority re real estate.* The "authority" is that which is granted for independent administration of estates. This means that court approval is not required for ordinary property transactions restructuring the estate and readying it for final distribution as per the will. Ordinary prudence and verifiable accounting are required. Self-dealing and unauthorized access to the decedent's estate are prohibited.

In Figure 10.2, we presented less than 20% of the California form DE-111. There are numerous other comparable forms in check-the-box fashion (75 in all!). It is not our intention to reveal all 75 of such forms. But we will at least mention a few others, to help you understand the essentials of the probate process.

Starting the Process

All probate forms in California start with a large block of white space across the top, with the words:

Attorney or Party Without Attorney
(Name, address, and phone number)

The implication in this wording is pretty clear. No attorney is needed if the "party without attorney" is the will-appointed executor of the decedent's estate. There is also another block of white space for entering the name of the decedent. This should be the exact name that appears on the decedent's last will, in which the executor is named.

A probate case is opened by depositing the original will plus its codicils (amendments), if any, with the clerk of the court, Probate Division. Immediately after its being receipt-stamped by the clerk, request at least one certified copy of it. There will be a fee involved. The executor must keep the certified copy of the will in his possession at all times. It signifies one's authority as executor, but it is not a judicial blessing. To acquire this blessing, certain probate forms have to be filed.

For California purposes, the following preprinted forms are required for starting the probate process:

1. Petition for Probate
2. Notice of Death and of Petition to Administer Estate
3. Order for Probate
4. Letters (Testamentary)

These forms are prepared by the executor/petitioner and are signed in the designated places. All of these forms have to be procured, and studied carefully, before completing them. These are the "papers" that you have to file with the probate clerk, at which time a Case Number is assigned.

The Petition for Probate form is your leadoff challenge. Make sure you X the box: ☐ *Probate of Will and for Letters Testamentary*, and the box: ☐ *Authorization to Administer under the Independent Administration of Estates Act.* Where requested by the form, enter such specifics as: (1) date and place of death; (2) domicile at that time; (3) estimated gross value of estate (with particular indication of the real property portion); (4) all close family members and heirs; and (5) other names, ages, relationships, and addresses of all other persons named in the will. When this petition form is complete, it has to be signed: *Under penalty of perjury.*

The Notice of Death and of Petition is the public notice that has to be given to all heirs, beneficiaries, creditors, contingent creditors, and other persons having a financial interest in the decedent's estate. The notice contains preprinted instructions to those who object, to those who are creditors, and to those who wish to examine the court-filed papers. There is space on the notice for entering the petition hearing date, time, and place. This space is filled in by the court clerk. See Figure 10.3.

The Notice of Death, etc. is mailed to heirs and beneficiaries, and published in a newspaper of general circulation where the decedent was domiciled. When this is done, and when the proper receipts are in hand, fill out the Order for Probate and the Letters (Testamentary) forms. These forms must be in the clerk's hands before the court hearing takes place. If there are no or minimal objections to the Petition for Probate, the judge signs the Order confirming the executor's appointment and his authority to act independently. The probate clerk signs the Letters (Testamentary) and affixes the court's seal to it. These "Letters" are a form of power of attorney after death, which empower the executor to do whatever is necessary to manage the estate.

Back in Figure 10.1, we presented a functional overview of how the process works, from beginning to end. If the indicated matters in Figure 10.1 make you feel a bit queasy, contact a paralegal service

Name & Address of Petitioner Name & Address of Superior Court Name of Decedent	For Court Use
NOTICE OF DEATH AND OF **PETITION TO ADMINISTER ESTATE**	**Case Number:** _____

1. To all heirs, bebeficiaries, creditors, contingent creditors, and persons who may be otherwise interested in the will or estate of _____
   _____

2. A petition has been filed by _____
   requesting appointment as personal representative to administer the estate of the decedent.

3. The petition requests authority to administer independently of court supervision.

4. A hearing on the petition will be held on

(date)	_(time)_	_(room)_	_(place)_

5. IF YOU OBJECT . . . , you should. . .
6. IF YOU ARE A CREDITOR . . . you must . . .
7. YOU MAY EXAMINE the file kept by the court
8. YOU MAY FILE a request for special notice . . . of estate assets. . . and of accounts and reports . . .

CLERK'S CERTIFICATE OF POSTING
_____

PROOF OF SERVICE BY MAIL
_____

HEIRS & BENEFICIARIES TO WHOM NOTICE MAILED

_____   _____

_____   _____

Fig. 10.3 - Abridged Format for Notice of Death and of Petition

in your area. Use your phone book or search the internet. A *paralegal* is a person trained in the nomenclature and preparation of legal forms, but cannot practice law. Absent any belligerent or contentious beneficiaries threatening you, there is no practice of law in the Figure 10.1 depiction.

Taking Possession of Estate

With Letters Testamentary, a nonattorney executor can go about the business of taking possession of the decedent's estate: real, tangible, intangible, and personal. This means notifying all persons or entities holding any of the decedent's property to turn it over to the executor. The purpose for doing so is to inventory and appraise it, and to restructure it (liquefy it) as necessary. To do this, you need to establish a separate bank account in the name of the decedent as: ***Estate of***_____. All monies that you receive and all expenses that you pay must go through this one account. Included in the term "expenses" are creditor claims, administrative costs, and applicable taxes. When all executor activities are complete, a "final accounting" will be required.

When the executor is issued Letters by the court clerk, there will be an accompanying: ***Order Appointing Inheritance Tax Referee***. This Order gives the name, address, and telephone number, with instructions . . . *to fix the clear market value of the property of said estate*. This includes inventory and appraisement of real property, investment holdings, business interests, promissory notes, bank accounts, etc. Items of household furniture, furnishings, and personal clothing are estimated. Works of art, antiques, collectibles, vehicles, equipment, etc. are appraised by specialists. The court-appointed appraiser gathers all of the pertinent data, then prepares a summary report to the probate court. A certified copy is sent to the executor. For different state laws, different inventory and appraisement procedures apply.

While the appointed referee (property appraiser) is doing his or her tasks, the executor has related tasks to perform. The executor must contact all creditors, all beneficiaries, and all others who either owe money to the estate or who perform services for it. These contacts and responses should be documented at each step of the way. With the exception of high-valued real estate, investment holdings, and business enterprises, most all other property items should be liquefied (i.e., either sold or given directly to designated recipients). From these estate funds, all legitimate debts, taxes, expenses, and costs have to be paid. One must do this dispensing — **and document it** — whether an estate is probated or not.

Meaning of "Independent Administration"

The Independent Administration of Estates Act was enacted in California in 1974. It appears in the California Probate Code at Sections 10400 through 10592. Selected excerpts from these numerous sections reveal that "full authority" means that—

> *Upon obtaining authority to administer the estate under this article, the executor . . . shall not be required to obtain judicial authorization, approval, confirmation, or instructions, . . . with respect to any actions during the course of the administration of the estate. . . . When no hearing is required because the executor or administrator does not seek court supervision of an action or proposed action, no publication . . . shall be required.* [The term "publication" means in the legal notices section of a general area newspaper.]

With authority for independent administration, the executor has legal power to do most anything and everything that is necessary in order to pursue the distributive intentions of the testator. No court supervision is required. This kind of unsupervised authority, however, carries with it certain implied responsibilities. The executor cannot be careless and cavalier. For example, he cannot sell a referee-appraised $1,000,000 parcel of real estate to himself, to a close friend, or to a favored beneficiary for $698,750. Therefore, situations can arise where the better part of wisdom is to seek court supervision, whether required or not. This is called: *advisory supervision*. It protects the executor against subsequent accusations of wrongdoing or misconduct.

Advisory supervision is indicated in the following situations:

1. Personal property items which will depreciate or perish rapidly in value if held to time of settlement.
2. Leasing real property for a term in excess of one year.
3. Completing any contract entered into by the decedent to convey real or personal property.
4. Continuing any unincorporated business or venture of the decedent, for more than six months.
5. The payments and terms of any "family allowance" paid from the estate.
6. Investing funds of the estate in other than federally insured bank and savings accounts, and government securities.
7. Borrowing money or executing a mortgage or deed of trust or giving other security.
8. The sale, exchange, option to buy, or encumbrance of property for the personal benefit of the executor and/or others.
9. When complaints or objections are raised by any heir or beneficiary whether credible or not, if made in writing.
10. Allowance of executor fee, settlement of accounts, final distribution to heirs and beneficiaries, and discharge of executor when estate is closed.

For these and similarly related matters, the executor prepares his own petition forms. The general arrangement of such a petition is presented in Figure 10.4. We call this figure a "blank" form. This is because its main body is devoid of any checkboxes. (The checkboxes in the heading are our version of a short title for the petition.)

The paragraphs: *Petitioner Requests* and *Petitioner States* (in Figure 10.4) are filled in by the executor/petitioner in his own words. To do this, he must present specific facts and circumstances that are directly pertinent to the decedent's estate. This includes distributee names and their respective sharing of transactional proceeds. In other words, all persons having a financial interest in the estate (heirs, beneficiaries, others) must be identified.

Those having a financial interest in the estate must also be notified. This is done by a private (not public) notice for which (in California) a preprinted form is available. This form is titled:

```
_____
        PETITIONER
  Name _____          For Court Use
  Address _____

  _____
  PETITIONER
              SUPERIOR COURT OF _____ (state) _____
                     COUNTY OF _____
                      Case No. _____

  _____ ESTATE OF _____
                                         PETITION FOR
  _____
                            ☐ Approval of Sale of Personal Property
  _____
                            ☐ Authority to Sell Securities

                            ☐ Confirmation of Sale of Real estate

                            ☐ Confirmation of Advice Given

                            ☐ Other

  Petitioner Requests _____
  _____ (brief statement of what petitioner wants court to do) _____


  Petitioner States    _____
  _____ (brief statement of facts upon which to base court decision) ____


  I declare under penalty of perjury that the foregoing, including
  any attachments, is true and correct.

  Executed on _____ (date) _____ at _____ (city & state) _____

  _____       _____
   (typed or printed name)          (signature)
```

Fig. 10.4 - "Blank" Format for Obtaining Court Supervision

Notice of Hearing (Probate). This form is mostly of blank space for entering the particulars of the hearing, its date and place, proof of service by mail, and name and address of each person to whom notice was mailed.

There is a special preprinted probate form (in California) when selling real property. It is titled: *Petition for Confirmation of Sale of Real Property*. It has approximately 30 checkboxes for indicating: (a) description of property sold, (b) its appraisal value and selling price, (c) manner and terms of sale, (d) commissions and expenses paid, and (e) reason for sale. If, at the hearing on the sale, there are any objections, comments, or suggestions, the judge addresses them, then signs a preprinted form: *Order Confirming Sale of Real Property*. The Order confirms that: (a) good reason existed for the sale, (b) the sale was fairly conducted, (c) the sale price was 90% or more of its officially appraised value, (d) the petitioner/executor delivered conveyance of title to the purchaser, and (e) the broker's commission is approved. From this point on, any objections or complaints by heirs or beneficiaries are moot.

Final Accounting & Disposition

Irrespective of having independent administration authority, a final accounting and distribution of the estate has to be made. There are three aspects for finalizing an estate. One is a summary accounting to the distributees of dollars in and dollars out. Two, is a summary accounting of the legal duties of the executor. And, three, a request is made for executor compensation and release from further duties.

The "final accounting" to the distributees is strictly a financial statement. It starts with a listing of the assets (and their values) of the gross estate at time of death. Any transformation and liquidation (conversion to money) is explained. All debts, expenses, and taxes payable by the estate are listed as subtractions from the gross estate. A *contingency holdback* amount is established (for unforeseen post-final claims), after which a distributable amount is shown. Of this distributable amount, each distributee's share is computed by using the precise language cited in the will.

The "legal duties" accounting is a listing of said duties and their dates of completion in a *Petition for Final Distribution* filed with the probate court. Included in such a petition are—

- Residence and date of death of decedent
- Date will admitted to probate
- Date Letters issued and confirmation of executor
- Date Notice to Creditors published
- Disposition of creditor claims
- Date inventory and appraisement filed
- Description of all taxes paid
- Listing of all debts and expenses paid
- Estimation of closing costs (contingency holdback)
- Listing of distributees and their respective sharing

The petition may also include a request for Waiver of Accounting to the court (as authorized by independent administration), a request for remuneration to the executor, and a request for release from further executor duties.

The whole idea behind this "final petition" is to give all persons who have a legitimate financial interest in the decedent's estate one last opportunity to be heard in court. If no such persons appear (as is most often the case), the judge signs an executor-prepared: *Judgment Directing Final Distribution and Waiver of Account.* An outline of the petition requirements and of the judgment order are given in each state's probate code. Both the petition and order are necessary documents to include in a permanent file on the deceased person.

To whom is this permanent file entrusted?

Answer: The primary distributee. Said person would most likely be: (a) the surviving spouse, (b) one or more adult children, or (c) the trustee of the family trust. The real virtue of the probate process is assurance to critics that things were done right. Except for intentional fraud, the executor can no longer be held liable.

11

THE TAXATION PROCESS

After Death, Taxation Is A Clearing Up Process So That The Recipients Of A Decedent's Estate Acquire Money And Property, Tax Free. There Are Two Principles Involved: INCOME Taxation And TRANSFER Taxation. At The Federal Level, Income Taxation Is Addressed On Form 1040 (For Individuals) And On Form 1041 (For Estates). Estates Earn Income From Date Of Death To Date Of Asset Distribution. Transfer Taxation Applies To The Value Of Assets (In EXCESS Of $1,000,000 To $3,500,000) Transferred By Gift, By Estate, And By Generation Skipping. All Such Transfers Coalesce Into One Tax Accounting Form 706 At Time Of Death.

Death and taxes; you know the story. You cannot avoid them. But there *is* a difference. Taxes can go on for a year or two after death. Taxes due but unpaid at time of death are not forgiven. This means that all prior tax returns that should have been filed, but were not, have to be reconstructed and addressed. In fact, there's a whole world of after-death taxation that has to be settled before any distributee receives his or her share of the decedent's estate.

The goal of the after-death taxation process is to settle all applicable taxes by paying them out of the estate, before passing money and property to the distributees. By so doing, money and property pass to the distributees tax free. Once each distributee takes possession of his or her share, any taxes accruing and due thereafter are borne by each distributee himself or herself.

The after-death taxation process consists primarily of inquiry, computation, and settlement. There are five specific branches of this effort, namely:

1. Personal income taxes due but unpaid at time of death.

2. Income taxes accruing by the estate during its process of administration.

3. Transfer taxes imposed on large estates ($3 million or so) for the privilege of passing money and property tax free.

4. Business taxes due (on partnerships and corporations) but unpaid at time of death.

5. Business taxes accruing during estate administration or pending sale of business (whichever is sooner).

As you know, there are federal taxes, state taxes, local taxes, and, possibly, foreign taxes that have to be addressed. For each taxing jurisdiction, there are different versions of income taxes, property taxes, sales taxes, employment taxes, employer taxes, and excise taxes (on fuel, firearms, heavy duty trucks, alcohol, tobacco, etc.). Obviously, we cannot address all of these taxes. But we can generalize them by focusing primarily on the federal taxation process associated with dying.

Accordingly, in this chapter, we want to acquaint you with the after-death chores associated with Form 1040 (for individuals), Form 1041 (for estates), and Form 706 (for asset transfers). We want to do this as though you were the executor of a decedent's estate. Whenever after-death taxation is involved, it is the executor who has sole responsibility for addressing and paying all proper taxes. Professional assistance in this regard may be sought. This assistance should include inquiry into those business activities in which the decedent participated, and advising the executor whether the decedent's business interests should be retained or sold. Much tax accounting and transformation of a decedent's estate are required, before distributions of money or property can be made to designated recipients. Estate administration matters always come first.

Start with Form SS-4

Purely by operation of law, when a person dies an estate is created. Other than a death certificate, no formal documentation is required. The "estate" consists of all that the decedent owned at time of his/her death: money, property, and liabilities, personal and otherwise. The estate can generate income as though the decedent were still alive.

The moment any income is generated, whether by a living person or by his/her estate, there is a reporting requirement to the IRS. It is the *payer* of that income who does the reporting. When the person is alive, the payer reports to the IRS using the social security number (SSN) of the person. But when that person dies, his/her SSN is no longer tax valid. Now, what does the payer of income do?

Enter, now, IRS **Form SS-4**. This form is titled: *Application for Employer Identification Number* (EIN). Do not let the word "Employer" throw you. The parenthesized subcaption instructions make it clear that the form is intended for use by estates, trusts, churches, corporations . . . "and others," as well as for employers of living persons. The reporting number being requested (EIN) is a Tax ID comparable to an SSN. An EIN is required when reporting to the IRS income generated by a nonperson, whatever the form of such entity may be. A decedent's estate clearly qualifies as a nonperson entity. While a trust also qualifies as a nonperson, an estate EIN is required before a trust EIN can be activated.

Form SS-4 is a "check-the-box" type EIN application form. Other than heading lines for name, address, etc., it consists of 16 checkboxes for: *Type of entity*, 9 checkboxes for: *Reason for applying*, and 12 checkboxes for: *Principal activity*. For type of entity, check ☒ *Estate* (*SSN of decedent*) _____.   For reason for applying, check ☒ *Other*: *decedent's date of death* _____.
For principal activity, check ☒ *Other*: *decedent's estate*.

The *How to Apply* instructions accompanying Form SS-4 say—

You can apply for an EIN online, by telephone, by fax, or by mail. Use only one method for each entity so you do not receive more than one EIN for an entity.

Application by telephone is the most helpful way. The IRS phone number, hours (7:30 a.m. to 5:30 p.m.) and other directions are in the instructions to the form. You'll be talking to a human person who will ask questions about various line numbers and checkboxes on the form. The expectation is that you will have completed the form as much as you can, before phoning. If you respond adequately, you'll be voice assigned an EIN on the spot. You'll be instructed to enter the phone-assigned number in the upper right-hand corner of your own proposed SS-4. You'll be directed to convey this EIN to all who pay income to the estate: interest, dividends, capital gains, rents, royalties, and so on.

Information Returns: Forms 1099

The IRS has designed a whole series of information returns called "1099s". These are not tax returns per se; they provide income-reportable information which a recipient uses to prepare his own tax return. There are approximately 33 such information forms, 16 of which are specifically described as "Form 1099" and 17 of which carry other form numbers and letters.

Who prepares the 1099 series of forms and sends them to the IRS for its computer-matching programs?

Answer: The **payer** of money or property (designated by its fair market value). Copies of each payer-prepared form are earmarked as follows:

Copy A — For IRS
Copy B — For Recipient
Copy D — For Payer

The recipient of Copy B can be a living person, a decedent's estate, a business entity, or a family trust.

In order for the IRS to process any of the 1099 series of forms, the payer is mandated by the IRS to acquire from the recipient (of money or property) his, her, or its Tax ID. For a decedent's estate, its Tax ID is that IRS-assigned EIN discussed above. There is a penalty against the payer for not requesting the EIN. There is also a penalty against the estate for not providing the EIN, once it has been assigned. There is a further penalty against the estate for not applying for an EIN before the first dollar of reportable income accrues to the estate. There is still another penalty if the estate does not report on its tax return the 1099 amount reported by the payer to the IRS.

Virtually without exception, at some point during its administration an estate earns income. For example, simply holding stock and securities can produce income in the form of dividends and capital gain distributions. When selling stock by the estate, the gross proceeds from the sale become reportable income. The same is true when the estate earns interest, rents, royalties, and other forms of income. When real property is sold, its gross proceeds are reported to the IRS. These and other forms of "1099" reporting require constant vigilance by the executor of the estate.

The more common 1099 reportings that an executor should be aware of are—

1099-B	:	Proceeds from Broker Transactions
1099-DIV	:	Dividends and Distributions
1099-INT	:	Interest Income
1099-MISC	:	Miscellaneous Income (rents, royalties, nonemployee compensation, and other)
1099-OID	:	Original Issue Discounts (federal bonds)
1099-R	:	Distributions from Pensions, Annuities, Retirement Plans, Insurance Contracts, etc.
1099-S	:	Proceeds from Real Estate Transactions

There is a point that we are getting at here. It is that once a decedent's estate is identified with an EIN, all payers of money or property to the estate must enter that EIN on each applicable 1099 form. The estate's EIN is entered in the 1099 box labeled: *RECIPIENT'S identification number*. This is immediately followed by the recipient's name: *Estate of JOHN J. JONES*, c/o the name and address of the executor. The amounts reported on all types of

1099 forms must cross-match with corresponding entries on the estate's income tax return.

Form 1040 vs. Form 1041

Not all executors fully understand the concept and role of an estate's income tax return. Said return is **Form 1041**. This form is titled: *U.S. Income Tax Return for Estates and Trusts.* The distinction as an estate return is by checking the box: ☒ *Decedent's estate.* Once this box is checked, Form 1041 becomes the counterpart to Form 1040: *U.S. Individual Income Tax Return.* There are similarities between these two returns with respect to certain types of income and deductions. But there are major dissimilarities as well.

For example, the initial income entry line on Form 1040 is captioned: *Wages, salaries, tips, etc.* Elsewhere, there are income entry lines for alimony received, IRA distributions, pensions and annuities, unemployment compensation, social security benefits, and other earned income types Collectively, these sources are called: *personal service income.* There is no provision whatever for entering personal service income on Form 1041. With respect to interest, dividends, capital gain or loss, business income or loss, rents, and royalties, etc., there is near-identicalness of nonpersonal service income on Forms 1040 and 1041.

To understand the Form 1040/Form 1041 distinction better, it is helpful to think of Form 1040 as a living person's return. The moment that person dies, Form 1040 is no longer proper. Nor is it proper to continue using the deceased person's SSN. Therefore, the first dollar of nonpersonal service income generated after death is NOT reported on Form 1040. It is reported on Form 1041. To do so, a new Tax ID is required. Hence, the application for, and the IRS assignment of, an EIN.

In Figure 11.1, we try to portray the 1040/1041 distinctions for you. Tax functionally, there is a sharp transition: 1040 with SSN, death, then 1041 with EIN. Theoretically, the contrast is simple enough but in practice there is much confusion.

Despite executors' efforts requesting payers to adjust their internal computer programs to use the estate's EIN instead of the

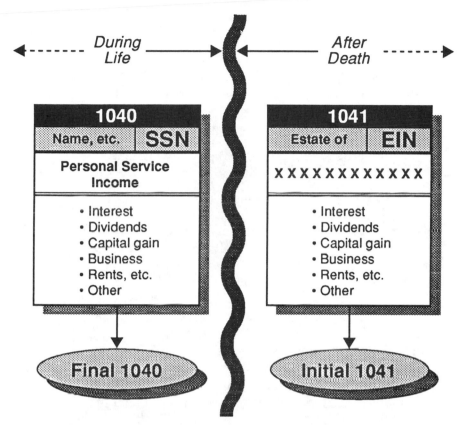

Fig. 11.1 - Distinguishing Features: Forms 1040 vs. 1041

decedent's SSN, many payers simply refuse to do so. Those payers who agree to do it, will only do it after the end of a calendar quarter, or after the end of the calendar year. The result often is that payer information that should have been reported to the IRS under an EIN is reported under a SSN . . . and vice versa. Just be aware of this.

In most cases, if you report all SSN-1099 information on Form 1040, and all EIN-1099 information on Form 1041, the IRS will accept the reality of the situation. The two most notable exceptions are Forms 1099-B (broker transaction) and 1099-S (sale of real property). Box 1 in each of these two forms calls for: *Date of sale or exchange*. An after-death transaction cannot be reported on Form 1040. Otherwise, both the 1040 and 1041 are due on or before April 15 following the year of death.

Death Year 1040 "Final"

When a person dies, his/her executor has to file a "final" Form 1040 for the year of death of that person. The purpose is to clear the IRS data bank of the SSN of the deceased person. "How is this done?" you may ask.

There is no "Final" checkbox on Form 1040 (as there is on Form 1041). Because so, the executor types or handprints in the white space at the very top of Form 1040 the wording—

FINAL RETURN. T/P Deceased _____*(date)*_____ .

The "T/P" is for taxpayer, if single. If married, T/P (H) is used for deceased husband, whereas T/P (W) is used for deceased wife. The surviving spouse is unaffected by either head notation.

We suggest using bold red lettering. You want to get the IRS's attention and put it on notice to search its data bank for any unfiled tax returns or any unpaid taxes by the decedent. Meanwhile, as executor, inquire among close family members regarding prior tax records of the decedent. You want to clear up any and all Federal tax matters outstanding. Do so likewise for state income tax filings. Also do so for any other decedent-relevant tax matters, especially those of a business type where the penalties can be brutal.

When a taxpayer dies, his/her final return is called a "short year" return. It is "short" in the sense that it covers less than 365 days of income generation. It may be short by anywhere from as little as one day to as many as 364 days. The length of shortness doesn't really matter so long as all payer reported information with the decedent's SSN is included. If the decedent was married, there, of course, would be no short year for the surviving spouse.

Whether single or married, we urge getting the decedent's final 1040 prepared and filed by no later than February 15 (following the death year). There are so many other after-death tax matters to address. If all Copy Bs of payer reportings have not been received by January 31 (the required date), contact the delinquent payer(s) and request the information by phone or fax. As executor, you simply MUST clear the final 1040 before going on to other tax matters, such as to Form 1041.

Short Span of Estate 1041

Form 1041, recall, is the *income* tax return for a decedent's *estate*. Its applicability is relatively short in duration: one to two years on average; three years at most. Once the estate is settled and distributed to its designated recipients, any income generated thereafter is tax reported by those recipients.

To accommodate a 1041's relative shortness of use time, the head portion of a 1041 displays the following three checkboxes (among others):

☐ *Initial return*   ☐ *Final return*   ☐ *Amended return*

Close by are such required short-line entries as:

EIN _____, *Date entity created*_____, and *Number of Schedules K-1 attached*_____.

The "date entity created" is the date of death of the decedent. As pointed out previously, an estate is an entity created by operation of law when someone dies.

In the death year itself, the box ☒ *Initial return* would be checked. If death occurred early in the year and if the estate were settled before the end of that year, the box ☒ *Final return* would also be checked. Otherwise, the final return checkbox would be X-ed one or two years after death. If a final return were signified and it later turned out that, unexpectedly, additional payer reported EIN income was being reported, the box ☒ *Amended return* would be checked. In other words, there is more flexibility and latitude when preparing Form 1041 than when preparing Form 1040. This greater latitude derives largely from the fact that no personal service income is reported on Form 1041.

With respect to nonpersonal service income, many of the same 1040 schedules may also be attached to Form 1041. This is particularly true of Schedule B (1040): *Interest and Ordinary Dividends*; Schedule C (1040): *Business Income or Loss*; Schedule

E (1040): *Rents, Royalties, and Partnerships*; Schedule F (1040): *Farm Income or Loss*; and Form 4797: *Ordinary Gain or Loss*.

Although analogous to Schedule D (1040): **Capital Gain or Loss**, there is a separate and different Schedule D (1041). This difference is due to the required separation of net capital gain from net capital loss. Only net gain can be passed through to the beneficiaries of the estate. Net loss is retained by the estate itself. When the checkbox ☒ *Final return* is checked, all accumulated losses in the estate then pass through to its beneficiaries.

Role of Schedule K-1

After all 1041 income is totaled and the allowable deductions are subtracted, a net distributable **income** is established. Who gets this income? The decedent's 1040 cannot get it because it accrued after his/her demise. The answer, therefore, is: Either the surviving spouse, if any, gets it or the decedent's surviving heirs get it.

Enter now the role of **Schedule K-1 (1041)**. This 1041 schedule is titled: **Beneficiary's Share of Income, Deductions, Credits, etc.** Note the singular possessive. A K-1 is prepared separately for each beneficiary who is a living person. The K-1 is functionally comparable to a Form 1099. It is an *information return*. The information is reported to the IRS under each beneficiary's Tax ID (SSN). The K-1 is designed so that each specific pass-through item is directed onto each corresponding schedule that attaches to each recipient's own Form 1040. The tax wisdom of the pass-through process is depicted in our Figure 11.2

If *all* of the beneficiaries assert that they do not want the involvement of a K-1, there is an option. The estate can pay the tax. (The K-1 tax rates are higher than those for individuals.) When the estate pays the tax, the after-tax income can be passed through to the beneficiaries tax free. No Schedules K-1 are then required.

Transfer Taxation: 3 Kinds

Whereas income taxation pertains to the generation of income from property being held by the estate, transfer taxation applies to the conveyance of that property to its beneficiaries. Let us explain.

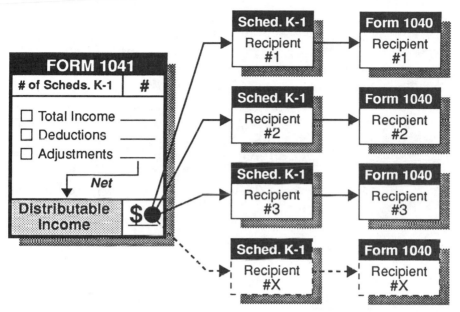

Fig. 11.2 - The Income Distribution Role of Schedules K-1 (Form 1040)

Most every person is accustomed to income taxation, but not many are aware of, nor understand the purpose of, transfer taxation. Said tax is imposed for the privilege of transferring money or property to others gratuitously. A gratuitous transfer is characterized by there being no obligation whatsoever to the transferor by the transferee. There is no loan repayment; no services to be performed; no consideration to be paid. Furthermore, the recipient gets the money or property tax free. If there is any tax to be paid, it is paid by the transferor.

Why is there a transfer tax?

Let's think about this for a moment. If the transfer of money or property were a *business* transaction, there would be some tax liability involved. Either the transferor, transferee, or both would pay a tax. Any form of tax means revenue to government. A gratuitous transfer provides no comparable revenue. Hence, to partially fill the void, a transfer tax is imposed.

There are three kinds of gratuitous transfers. There are: (1) a gift transfer (during life), (2) an estate transfer (after death), and (3) a generation-skipping transfer (after skipping over the first generation down). In all these cases, after statutory exclusions, a tax applies. The maximum rate of this tax is between 35% and 45% depending on the year of transfer and on the politics of Congress.

The imposition of transfer tax is set forth in three separate sections of the Internal Revenue Code, namely:

Gift Tax. IRC Sec. 2501(a) — *A tax . . . is hereby imposed . . . on the transfer of property by gift . . . by any individual, resident or nonresident.*

Estate Tax. IRC Sec. 2001(a) — *A tax is imposed on the transfer of the taxable estate of every decedent who is a citizen or resident of the U.S.*

GST Tax. IRC Sec. 2601(a) — *A tax is hereby imposed on every generation-skipping transfer* [to a natural person two or more generations below (that) of the transferor].

Before any transfer tax is imposed, there is a statutory exclusion amount. In the case of gifts, there is a $1,000,000 (1 million) lifetime exclusion. In the case of estate transfers, the exclusion ranges from $1,500,000 to $3,500,000 (1.5 to 3.5 million) depending on year of death. In the case of GSTs, the same exclusion applies as for estate transfers. Each exclusion is applied independently of the others.

The net effect is that the transfer tax applies only to above-modest asset transfers. As a broad generalization, the term "above modest" means more than $3,000,000 (3 million). Hence, the transfer tax is **not** an omnipresent tax as is the income tax. It only applies to the transfer of assets: not to the income from those assets. As above indicated, income taxation is a separate process.

Form 706: "Yes" or "No"

Because of the transfer tax concept, one of the most comprehensive and intimidating of all IRS forms is **Form 706**. It is officially titled: ***U.S. Estate (and Generation-Skipping Transfer)***

Tax Return. We prefer a shorter title such as: *U.S. Estate Transfer Tax Return*. Our title, we believe, puts the emphasis where it belongs. It is a TRANSFER tax return of an estate, in contrast to an INCOME tax return for the same estate. There is no correlation whatsoever between Form 706 and Form 1041. One's "estate" is the summation of his/her marketable assets reconstructed at time of death.

Form 706 is an all inclusive reconstruction of a decedent's assets: during life, upon death, and after death. A general overview of its contents is presented in Figure 11.3. The basic form itself, without attachments of any kind, is 40 pages or so in length. Yes, 40 pages! Not all of the schedules listed in Figure 11.3 will apply to every decedent. Nevertheless, Figure 11.3 gives you an idea of how extensive the coverage is in Form 706. Please, at least, skim read the list of schedules and pause for a moment at Schedule G: *Transfers During Decedent's Life* (gifts) and Schedule R: *Generation-skipping Transfer Tax*. This is what we mean by an all-inclusive reconstruction of an estate.

When are the preparation and filing of Form 706 required?

Answer: The instructions to Form 706 say—

For decedents dying in ___(year)___, Form 706 must be filed by the executor for the estate of every U.S. citizen or resident whose gross estate, plus adjusted taxable gifts . . ., is more than—

- $1,000,000 for death years 2002 and 2003;
- $1,500,000 for death years 2004 and 2005;
- $2,000,000 for death years 2006, 2007, and 2008;
- $3,500,000 for death years 2009 and (who knows?).

The term: "plus adjusted taxable gifts" is mostly a red herring. It applies to those cumulative gifts made between 1977 and 2002. Gifts made in 2003 and thereafter are recaptured on Schedule G of Form 706. A filer is given the option of including *all* during-life transfers on Schedule G. Where such option is elected, there are no adjusted taxable gifts to be computed. Whatever gifts are on Schedule G are automatically included in the decedent's gross estate for Form 706 purposes. Any prior-to-death gift tax paid is credited against any subsequent estate tax.

Form 706 - United States Estate Tax Return		
Page	**Information Required**	
1.	Part 1 - Decedent & Executor: 10 entries	
	Part 2 - Computation of Tax: 25 lines	
2.	Part 3 - Executor Elections: 4 items	
	Part 4 - Decedent & Beneficiary Information - 5 descriptive entries	
3.	Part 4 - (Continued) 11 "yes / no" Questions	
	Part 5 - Recapitulation: Assets & Deductions: 23 lines	
4.	Schedule A	Real Estate
12.	Schedule B	Stocks & Bonds
13.	Schedule C	Mortgages, Notes, & Cash
15.	Schedule D	Insurance on Decedent's Life
17.	Schedule E	Jointly Owned Property
19.	Schedule F	Other Miscellaneous Property
21.	Schedule G	Transfers During Decedent's Life
	Schedule H	Powers of Appointment
22.	Schedule I	Annuities
23.	Schedule J	Funeral and Administration Expenses
25.	Schedule K	Debts of Decedent; Mortgages & Liens
26.	Schedule L	Losses of, and Claims Against Estate
27.	Schedule M	Bequests to Surviving Spouse
31.	Schedule O	Charitable & Public Gifts
32.	Schedule P	Credit for Foreign Death Taxes
	Schedule Q	Credit for Tax on Prior Transfers
33.	Schedule R	Generation-Skipping Tax
38.	Schedule T	Family-Owned Business Deduction
42.	Schedule U	Conservation Easement Exclusion
43.	Unlettered	Continuation of Any of the Above

Fig. 11.3 - General Overview / Contents of Form 706

To determine if Form 706 is a required filing, the executor has to prepare at least a worksheet for each of Schedules A, B, C, D, E, F, G, H and I: nine in all (as per Figure 11.3). This means reading the instructions to each of these schedules and making all entries thereon in draft form. If the total gross estate of these nine schedules is within 10% of the exclusion amounts above, then we say: "File Form 706." This is the case of where you file a return to prove that you did not have to file the return. If you file a not-required Form 706, it becomes an *Information Return*: not a tax return . . . because no tax is due.

When No Form 706 Required

Executors of modest estates (less than $1,500,000) tend not to take Form 706 seriously. They make an off-the-top-of-head estimate of what the decedent's gross estate may be. They low ball their estimates of asset values and immediately conclude that no Form 706 is required. They immediately distribute the assets to anxiously waiting and demanding distributees. The estate is then prematurely closed. There is a high degree of imprudence and risk in this cavalier approach.

One risk is the assumption that the IRS will not care, since no Form 706 is being filed. Another risk is the assumption that no recipient of tax-free assets would dare question the ethics and accounting practices of the executor. A third risk is that no state inheritance tax agency, which treats and computes transfer taxes differently from the IRS, will come forth with an accounting demand after all assets have been distributed.

There is also a fourth risk. If, for some out-of-the-woodwork reason, the IRS requests a Form 706 or an explanation for its nonfiling, or a state's inheritance tax is imposed, or a Form 1041 income tax filing is required, who pays these taxes?

Answer: The executor does! [IRC Section 2002.]

In another out-of-the-woodwork situation, what happens when a distributee sells a parcel of real property for $750,000 which he received from the executor tax free? Does he pay capital gain tax on the full $750,000 or on some lesser amount?

Answer: On some lesser amount . . . *provided* the executor conveys to the distributee authentic documentation on what the property was worth at date of death of the decedent. In other words, the "lesser amount" is the difference between the sales price of the property less its *tax basis* at time of death.

IRC Section 1014(a)(1) states rather succinctly that—

> *The basis of property in the hands of a person acquiring* [it]
> *from a decedent . . . shall, if not sold, exchanged, or otherwise*
> *disposed of before the decedent's death by such person, be—*
>
> *(1) the fair market value of the property at the date of the*
> *decedent's death.*

Here's where Schedule A: *Real Estate* of Form 706 comes in handy. Instructions to this schedule require that each property item thereon be described in some detail, and that its *value at date of death* be entered. The entered value must be supported by a professional appraisal with certification attached directly to Schedule A. If, in our $750,000 example above, the property was listed on Schedule A for $700,000, the taxable amount of capital gain would be $50,000 [750,000 – 700,000]. Otherwise, without the Schedule A (Form 706) documentation, the taxable capital gain to the distributee seller would be $750,000.

Are you getting our message? Our position is this. On matters of asset valuation at time of death, Schedules A through I of Form 706 should be completed diligently. This should be done irrespective of whether or not the official filing of Form 706 is required. The effort devoted to preparing these schedules will enable the executor to face all value challenges, whether by a taxing agency or by some disgruntled distributee.

12

WRITING YOUR OWN WILL

A Will, When Written By The Testator Himself/Herself, Is Not Forever Cast In Concrete. It Can Be Changed To Reflect Changes In Family Status, Financial Conditions, Property Holdings, And Intended Distributees. It Can Be Formulated On 3 To 5 Printed Pages Of Declaratory Text Comprising 9 To 12 Separately Numbered Paragraphs. With The Exception Of Surviving Spouse And Minor Children, A Will Writer Can "Give, Devise, And Bequeath" Much Or Little To Adult Recipients. A Will Starts With A Preamble And Ends With A Witness Paragraph. Two Witnesses Are Required Who Are Not Distributees Nor Are They Husband And Wife.

Our premise has always been: Every adult person needs a will; not every such person needs a trust. The concept of a will — leaving property to designated heirs and beneficiaries — goes back to biblical times. It is a fundamental and human right of ownership to designate who shall receive one's property upon his or her demise. A will is not an "entity" as is a trust. A will is a document expressing testamentary intent at time of death. Who better knows what this intent is than the owner and possessor of property?

In prior chapters, we tried to lay the foundation for distinguishing between the features of a will and those of a trust. The most distinguishing feature, we believe, is that whereas a will consists of some three to five pages of text, a trust consists of some 35 to 50 pages. This implies that a will is clearly the simpler document to prepare. Being simpler, a will can be prepared, changed, and rechanged as circumstances require. This means that working persons, those with young families, and those with modest estates (less than $1,500,000) can prepare their own wills without the need for an attorney.

Accordingly, in this, our last chapter, we want to provide you with samples of how a "simple will" can be self-prepared. Our goal is to provide sample paragraphs — with *fictitious* names, places, and property holdings — which you can use either directly or by modification to fit your own situation. We word these paragraphs based on many of the comments that we have made previously. If your particular situation is not befitting that of a simple will, we urge that you seek professional counseling.

Sample Preamble Wording

A preamble to a will is a self declaration by the testator that he has the requisite testamentary capacity to make a will. Such a declaration must be clear and unequivocal. It sets the stage for all that follows in the will.

The paragraph below is an illustrative example of what would likely constitute an acceptable will preamble in most states. This and other paragraph examples will be presented throughout this chapter purely for instructional purposes. One could use these examples to prepare the initial draft of his own will. Upon completion of the draft, one should review his entire will as a whole before finalizing, typing, and witnessing.

Let us assume that our testator is John Quincy Jones. It could be Mary Jane Morgan and the preamble wording would be the same. Thus—

LAST WILL AND TESTAMENT
OF
JOHN QUINCY JONES

I, JOHN QUINCY JONES, a resident of Redding, County of Shasta, State of California, being of sound and disposing mind and memory, and not acting under duress, menace, fraud, or undue influence of any person whomsoever, do make, publish, and declare this to be my Last Will and Testament, in the manner and form following, to wit:

A will, obviously, will consist of more than its preamble alone. It may comprise as few or as many paragraphic statements as the testator desires. There is no minimum length nor maximum length. A will should state what the testator wants to state: no more, no less. Distinctly separate paragraphs should be used. Care must be taken to make each paragraph serve a single purpose and stand by itself alone. This way, if a will is attacked, one paragraph could be invalidated, while the rest could remain intact and acceptable.

Regardless of the number of paragraphs in a will, each one should be separately numbered and separately referenced where applicable. The numbering should be: First, Second, Third . . . Ninth, or whatever. Almost any will, no matter how complex the testator's affairs, can be organized into multiple separate paragraphs functionally distinct from each other. Directness and clarity are the keys for doing so.

Revocation is "First"

To cover future bases and assure that mistakes of the past are erased, the very first paragraph in a will should be a revocation clause. Even if no prior will or testaments have been made, a revocation clause should be entered. This clears the table for a fresh start, as though the present will is one's first and only.

The revocation clause may be general, or it may be specific, or both. If a specific revocation is intended, it should follow the general revocation. The "specifics" refer to an actual prior testamentary document, its date, and its place of execution. Do not attach a copy of the former document; it will only lead to confusion.

Now, for an example, continuing with John Quincy Jones—

FIRST

I hereby revoke any and all former Wills, Codicils to Wills, and Testamentary Dispositions by me at any time heretofore made. (General) and

*I specifically revoke my former Will dated April 22, 1998
executed at Denver, Colorado.* (Specific)

A "codicil" is an amendment, supplement, or change to an
existing will, usually limited to one or two clarifications only. A
"testamentary disposition" refers to holographic wills, oral
promises, and other instances of prior testamentary intentions. One
can only revoke a revocable instrument.

One cannot revoke an *irrevocable* instrument, such as a trust
formed with life insurance, an annuity contract, a transfer by gift, or
an assignment to one's spouse or to charity. These and others tend
to be legal documents beyond the expertise of any ordinary testator.

To summarize the preamble and first paragraph features that we
have just discussed, we present Figure 12.1.

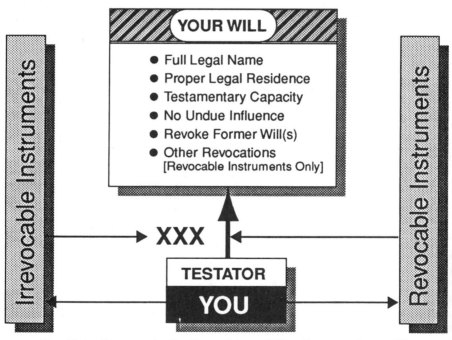

Fig. 12.1 - Features in the Preamble and First Paragraph to a Will

Declaration of Heirs: "Second"

Upon revoking any former will or testamentary instrument, the next paragraphic provision is a declaration of one's heirs. Descendants get priority over ascendants. Declaring all of one's rightful heirs does not mean that they will necessarily receive equal amounts of the testator's estate. If all are properly identified, the testator then has freedom to pick and choose those with whom he wants to share his estate, and to what degree.

In case one of the first-line heirs is deceased, the descendants of that heir should be identified. Again, this is for identity purposes only. Whether these second-line heirs share in the testator's estate is another matter.

One concern that frequently arises in the identification of heirs pertains to the spouses of any married children of the testator. Said spouses of married children are strangers in blood to the testator. They are not his natural heirs. If he desires to make provision for them, he can. If so, they become his named legatees, not his heirs.

Now, let us illustrate in declaratory words a situation that is fairly typical of an ordinary family unit not involved in divorce or remarriage. Take the case of John Quincy Jones (as before) who is married to Mary Jane (Morgan) Jones. Assume that John and Mary have three children: David, Jane, and Joseph. To place this situation in declaratory form, John's will might read—

SECOND

I hereby declare that I am married to MARY JANE (MORGAN) JONES, and that we have three children, namely: a son, DAVID MARK JONES, age approximately 30 years; a daughter, JANE ELIZABETH JONES, age approximately 20 years; and a son, JOSEPH SCOTT JONES, age approximately 10 years.

Correct full names are important to avoid mis-identities of persons with similar names. Identifying the relationship to the testator also helps avoid mis-identities. Giving approximate ages helps to distinguish between adults and minors. If the age of a minor child becomes a critical matter in estate distribution(s), that child's birth certificate can always be produced later.

There can be situations where the testator (John in the above) is divorced and has remarried, or one of his children is deceased, or one of his adult children is married or divorced. Addressing these situations is done in a replacement which is still enumerated as SECOND. We covered most of these possibilities back on pages 9-5 through the top portion of 9-9.

Appointment of Executor: "Third"

An executor has important duties to perform on behalf of the testator, after a testator deceases. As such, the executor becomes the *personal representative* of the testator for carrying out his/her distributive intent as expressed in the will. Because of the importance of these duties and their associated accounting chores, every testator should always have a list of candidate executors in mind. From this "mental list," one should nominate and appoint his/her own executor, rather than permitting the court to do so. Even when probate is required, the court having jurisdiction will, in most cases, confirm the will-appointed executor(s).

Prudence suggests that you nominate and appoint *two* executors. One should be successor to the other. They should *not* be co-executors. Co-executors (the "co" means equal) can create conflicts of authority at a time when conflicts cost money and delay. Your *successor* executor serves when and only when your first executor is unwilling or unable to serve.

To illustrate the appointment wording that might be appropriate to your will, consider the case of John Quincy Jones again. Recall that he is married to Mary, whose maiden name is Morgan. Mary has a brother, Gary Conrad Morgan, whom John wants to appoint as successor executor.

THIRD

I hereby nominate and appoint my wife, MARY, as Executrix of this my last Will and Testament, and direct that she shall be empowered to act as such without bond. In the event that my wife should predecease me or for any reason be unable or unwilling to act or continue as my Executrix, then I nominate and appoint my brother-in-law, GARY CONRAD MORGAN, as Executor to likewise act without bond.

In the event that the surviving spouse (Mary above) does not wish to serve as executrix, she can turn the matter completely over to the successor executor (Gary above). Or, as is often the case, Mary may feel that she wants assistance from Gary, but wants to retain the title of executrix. This she can do by signing all the necessary papers after Gary prepares them. Thus, Gary becomes her confidant and backup.

Ordinarily, the appointment of two executors in one's will is quite adequate. Reasonable flexibility can be achieved. However, if the testator is concerned about the imminent demise of his surviving spouse, or that the successor may prove disappointing, he can appoint some other relative, who is business seasoned, as *executor of last resort.*

Delegation of Powers: "Fourth"

There is little purpose in appointing an executor if you do not simultaneously delegate to him/her the necessary power to carry out your intentions. In the process of delegating adequate powers, you might also instruct your executor to accomplish your intentions within a specified lapse of time. This makes it clear to all concerned that you mean business. You do not want your estate affairs dragged on indefinitely. You want expeditious settlement.

Of course, you cannot empower your executor to do anything illegal. But you can certainly empower him to do everything necessary within the context of your own authority over your own property.

Even though it is not necessary to state so it is advisable to instruct your executor to pay all taxes, debts, and expenses applicable to your estate, prior to full and final distributions to your heirs and legatees. Laws beyond your testamentary powers require that death and all other taxes be paid; that all valid debts be paid; and that all reasonable expenses (fees) of administering your estate be allowed. Nevertheless, by specifically instructing your executor to take care of these matters first, your heirs and legatees are on notice to be patient: they will get their full share in due time.

FOURTH

I direct that my Executor or Executrix, whoever it may be, shall have full power to sell, exchange, rearrange, transfer, or otherwise dispose of as much of the property of my estate as he or she deems advisable and necessary, in order to distribute and settle my estate as directed herein, by independent administration without giving notice and without judicial accounting of any kind. I specifically direct that all taxes, debts, and expenses applicable to my estate be paid prior to final distributions, and that all assets be distributed and my estate be settled within nine (9) months of my demise, or, at the very latest, within 15 months of my demise.

In Paragraph Fourth above, note the clause: "by independent administration without giving notice and without judicial accounting." This is known as granting the *power* of independent administration. Except in the case of "advisory supervision" (by the court), no prior notice of your executor's intentions has to be given. To be most prudent, however, seek from the courts: *Letters Testamentary*. We described this process back on pages 6-6 through the top of 6-9.

The essence of power of independent administration is that your executor does not have to seek approval from an attorney, from a probate court (if any), or from any beneficiary of your estate, for conducting day-to-day transactional affairs. Except for certain activities, such as selling high-value real property, your executor is free to do those things that you want him to do, in order to carry out your distributive wishes.

That is, your executor can manage, control, sell, convey, divide, exchange, partition, encumber, lease, abandon, maintain, insure, and/or otherwise rearrange the assets of your estate. He can allow, pay, reject, contest, and/or compromise any claims by creditors or plaintiffs. He can file all necessary tax returns, pay all taxes and assessments, and pay all professional fees. He can collect and/or enforce collection of all monies and accounts due you at time of your demise. He can pay reasonable family allowances to your dependent survivors. In short, at his sole discretion, he can do most all things of a business/financial nature to settle your estate.

Declaration of Property: "Fifth"

The central purpose of any will is to dispose of one's property upon his demise. One can only direct the disposition of his own property; he cannot direct the disposition of someone else's property. Consequently, every testator must declare what property is his own and must identify it with reasonable certainty.

Consider, for example, a testator who was married at an early age and had no significant separate property of his own prior to marriage. Further, assume that he remained married throughout his adult life during which time he acquired no separate property by gift or by inheritance. Under these circumstances, his property declaration might read as—

FIFTH

I hereby declare that all of my property, both real and personal, tangible and intangible, of whatever kind or nature, wherever situated, is the marital property of my wife, MARY, and myself, regardless of the form in which the same may be presently held by us or either of us. I specifically declare that I have no separate property acquired before our marriage or during our marriage.

Suppose now that the testator above married later in life (for the first time). Suppose he had separate property worth about $125,000 before marriage and that during marriage he was gifted $100,000 from his father; and that later he inherited from his mother real property worth $580,000. Suppose he wanted to commingle his separate intangible property with his marital estate, but wanted to keep his inherited real property separate. This he can do. Accordingly, his property declaration might read as—

FIFTH

I hereby declare that prior to my marriage I had the sum of approximately $125,000 in my own right, and that shortly after my marriage I was gifted the sum of $100,000 from my father. These two separate amounts have been knowingly and purposefully commingled with my marital estate in joint tenancy with my wife, DOROTHY. In addition, I inherited from my late mother real property worth about $580,000. It is my intention to keep this inherited real property separate and apart from that of my marital estate with DOROTHY. With this one exception, I declare that all of my property, both real and personal, tangible and intangible, wherever situated, is the marital property of my said wife and myself, regardless of the form in which the same may be held by us or either of us.

In the case of divorces and remarriages, and widowers and widows remarrying, the decision to commingle or not to commingle, to gift or not to gift, presents a real dilemma. Much depends on the relative magnitudes of the separate assets, the number of children of each remarrying spouse and the ages of the remarrying spouses. Where prior-spouse children are involved and the remarrying spouses are past childbearing age, keeping the prior-marriage property separate is often desired.

Declaration of Gifts, etc.: "Sixth"

In a manner similar to declaration of one's property, a declaration of taxable gifts and of transfers for insufficient consideration should be made. A "taxable gift" is one for which IRS **Form 709** was filed, even though no actual tax was paid. A taxable gift is that amount which exceeds the annual exception of $11,000 per donor per donee. A "transfer for insufficient consideration" is when you sell or exchange property (usually among family members or close business associates) for less than its fair market value. Such a transaction is considered to be part sale and part gift. Many testators do not make these declarations because they do not understand why such are necessary.

A declaration of gifts and transfers comes under the tax theory of: *contemplation of death.* Contemplative transfers are more likely made by above-modest wealth testators. Their motivation is to reduce significantly their property holdings at time of death. The less property to be inventoried and appraised, the less tax considerations to be addressed. To counter this effort, the contemplation theory holds that if there is a flurry of gifts and transfers within three years of death, they are re-included back into the gross estate. Certain transfers more than three years back, if less than full-market-value-consideration paid, also are includible.

Consider, for example, a testator who has gifted a piece of real property to his son, Joseph. At about the same time, he has transferred shares in a mutual fund account to his daughter, Jane, and her two children. His declaratory paragraph might read as—

SIXTH

I hereby declare that I have gifted a parcel of land to my son, JOSEPH, valued at $125,000 on April 15, 2003, for which a gift tax return has been filed and annexed hereto. I also declare that on the same date I transferred $33,000 worth of shares in a mutual fund, namely THE ACORN FUND, INC. to my daughter, JANE, and her two children (my grandchildren), thereby gifting no more than $11,000 to each of three donees.

Suppose now that a testator had made a whole series of gifts over an extended period of his life. Suppose, too, that his gift tax returns were professionally prepared and cumulatively sequenced to each other. His appropriate declaratory paragraph might be—

SIXTH

I hereby declare that I have made a series of gifts, some outright and some with retained interests, to various heirs and legatees of mine, commencing on January 1, 2000. In each case, a gift tax return has been filed and will be filed as appropriate after the date hereof. Photocopies of said returns are annexed hereto. I specifically declare that I have made no

*transfers whatsoever for insufficient consideration, nor have I
received any such transfers from other persons.*

The annexing of gift tax returns to a will is express
manifestation of a disciplined state of mind. By documenting each
specific transfer date, you can negate any tax presumption that you
are engaged in rash or impulsive contemplation-of-death moves.

Bequests to Spouse: "Seventh"

If a testator is married, the expectation is that all marital property
will pass directly to his/her surviving spouse. This way, family
financial continuity is assured, whether the children are minors or
adults when one parent dies. There is no probate problem if the
marital property is held in joint tenancy, or as community property,
or as tenancy by the entirety (in noncommunity states). There is no
transfer tax problem either, so long as the property bequeathed to
spouse is no greater than $1,500,000 for death years 2004 and 2005,
or no greater than $2,000,000 for death years 2006, 2007, and 2008.

With the foregoing comments in mind, let us consider that John
is the testator and that Mary is the actuarially expected surviving
spouse. Accordingly, John's will bequest to his wife might read:

SEVENTH

*I hereby give, devise, and bequeath all of my estate (real,
tangible, intangible, and personal), of whatever kind or nature,
wherever situated, of which I may die possessed or to which
may be entitled at the time of my demise, to my wife, MARY, if
she survives me more than . . .*

Before any bequest to one's spouse can take effect, the decedent
spouse must be survived by his/her spouse. For various reasons,
there is always the prospect that both spouses could decease within a
short period of time of each other. Consequently, it is advisable to
include a "more than" certain number of days provision. The most
common provisions are 30, 60, or 90 days. Fewer than 30 days is
unrealistic, as is more than 90 days. A reasonable time is 60 days.

Within this time frame, the mental status of the surviving spouse should be sufficiently stabilized for going forward in life.

Another variant of the surviving spouse bequest is where the decedent spouse's estate may exceed the statutory exclusion for transfer tax purposes ($1,500,000+). In this case, the testator may want to create a *testamentary* trust to isolate the exclusion amount and protect it against re-inclusion in the surviving spouse's estate. He makes appropriate instructions in his will and, after his death, the executor would be empowered to create the trust.

Accordingly, the Paragraph Seventh might read as—

SEVENTH

In the event that my gross estate should exceed the federal statutory exclusion for my year of death, I direct that my executor shall be empowered to create and maintain an Exempt (or Bypass) Trust for such amount. As to all the rest and remainder of my estate, whether real, tangible, intangible, or personal, of whatever kind or nature, wherever situated, I give, devise, and bequeath it directly to my wife, MARY, if she survives me more than 60 days.

By this wording, an alert executor knows that the decedent spouse wants to accomplish two things. The decedent wants to expressly set aside the statutory exclusion amount. Doing so specifically prevents it from being re-included in the surviving spouse's estate upon her/his demise. The "all the rest and remainder" wording, whatever the actual amount may be, becomes an allowable *Marital Deduction* against the taxable estate of the decedent. The net, net result is: **no estate transfer tax** for the first decedent spouse's estate!

Common Disaster Clause: "Eighth"

For any marital deduction to take effect, the decedent must be survived by his/her spouse. If both spouses should die in a common disaster or under circumstances which make it impossible to establish by proof the order of their deaths, there is no surviving spouse. In this situation, differing state-law presumptions are made.

Applicable in many states is a presumption of survivorship under the Uniform Simultaneous Death Act. This Act presumes that each spouse is the survivor for disposing of his/her own property. This presumption automatically bars the marital deduction in those states which recognize the Act.

One's will can countermand any state-law presumption concerning the order of spousal deaths in a common disaster. In other words, if reciprocal (mirror) wills are written with identical presumptions and there indeed occurs a common disaster, the two wills cancel each other out as to who is the surviving spouse. Then neither one gets the marital deduction. This is good because if one spouse claims the deduction, the other must include the same amount in his or her estate. Canceling each other on this matter greatly simplifies the accounting for each spouse's estate.

Let us illustrate with reciprocal husband and wife wills as follows:

EIGHTH

Husband — *In the event that MARY and I should perish in a common disaster, or under circumstances that would make it impossible or extremely difficult to ascertain which of us died first, then it shall be presumed that I predeceased her.*

Wife — *In the event that JOHN and I should perish . . . then it shall be presumed that I predeceased him.*

Or, if there were expectation of surviving children, alternative wording could be—

EIGHTH

In the event that my wife, MARY, should not survive me more than 60 days, OR in the event that MARY and I should perish in a common disaster (in which case it shall be presumed that I predeceased her), OR in the event that MARY should predecease me, then all my net estate, in kind or value, after debts, expenses, and taxes, shall be distributed equally among my three children, DAVID, JANE, and JOSEPH.

Where direct bequests to children are made (as in paragraph "Eighth" above), their ages, character, and financial temperament are considerations. We addressed some of these matters back on page 9-9 (starting midway thereon) through Figure 9.3 on page 9-11. For children of ordinary intelligence, age 35 is considered as having attained financial maturity. A testator can bequeath directly to children of this age . . . and be done with it. It is towards younger children and those with special needs that bequests should be made with care. For this, young adults and spendthrift children come first to mind.

Young Adults & Spendthrifts: "Ninth"

The age of majority differs in various states, ranging from 16 to 21. For simplicity, we will treat the age of minority as being under 20 years. "Young adults," therefore, would range from 20 to 35. This is an age span of rapid changes in interests and financial needs. This is also the age span of normal marriage . . . and early divorce . . . and when infant grandchildren appear on the scene.

The simplest disbursement arrangement for young adult children is some form of **custodial trust**. This is an account set up with a financial institution of the testator's choice "in trust for" each child. No particular formality is required. Usually, an executor with Letters Testamentary and a photocopy of the pertinent will paragraph directing such arrangement are sufficient.

To highlight these points, let us consider a widow/widower parent with four adult children. Two are over 35 (Kenneth and Valerie) and two are under 35 (Robert and Constance). The bequests by such a parent might read as—

NINTH

I hereby give, devise, and bequeath all of my net estate, after applicable debts, expenses, and taxes, of whatever kind or nature, wherever situated, of which I may die possessed or entitled, to my four children as follows:

KENNETH	*20%}*	
VALERIE	*20%}*	*Total*
ROBERT	*30%}*	*100%*
CONSTANCE	*30%}*	

In the event that ROBERT or CONSTANCE should be of age less than 35 at the time of my demise, his or her share of my net estate shall be assigned to a separate Custodial Account with the PARAMOUNT MUTUAL FUND, which I have previously contacted. Accordingly, I hereby appoint VALERIE to be the fiduciary for ROBERT's account and KENNETH to be the fiduciary for CONSTANCE's account. Each fiduciary shall limit the withdrawals from each custodial account to $25,000 per year. As ROBERT and CONSTANCE each attains the age 35, his or her custodial account shall terminate and all remaining proceeds shall be lump-sum distributed.

As an alternative to the above paragraph, suppose it is clear to an elderly parent that one child, a son by the name of BOSWICK, is an incurable spendthrift. He is 45 years old, with no wife, no savings, no investments, and no property holdings of any kind. He has no job and no health insurance. He requires a protected source of funds for food, housing, medical, transportation, and other special needs.

One way to provide this protection is to establish a **testamentary trust** at the time of the parent's death. BOSWICK's intended estate could be placed in a designated financial institution with a conservative management history. The trustee should be a close family member who is **not** a brother or sister to BOSWICK. Accordingly, the situation could be addressed in a 5-part will paragraph which might read as—

NINTH

A. With respect only to my son, BOSWICK, I specifically direct that his share of my estate be liquidated and deposited in a Testamentary Trust with the WORLD CAPITAL MANAGE-MENT GROUP of Denver, Colorado. The type of account or accounts held in trust shall be at the discretion of the trustee.

B. The initial trustee of the trust shall be my brother, MICHAEL, and as successor trustee my nephew, WARREN. The trustee shall be entitled to a reasonable fee, if claimed.

C. The trustee shall distribute to BOSWICK, each month, a sum not less than $2,000 nor more than $3,000, the specific amount being at the sole discretion of the trustee. Other disbursements to BOSWICK shall be made only in the event of prudent necessity, such as (1) major medical, (2) hospitalization, (3) vehicular transportation, (4) equipment for a productive business, and (5) down payment on a personal residence.

D. The trust shall terminate when the total account balance diminishes below $20,000. At that point, all remaining funds shall be distributed to BOSWICK.

E. At all times during the existence of the trust, no portion of its principal or income shall be anticipated, assigned, or encumbered, or subject to any creditor's claims or to legal process prior to its actual receipt by BOSWICK.

With this kind of will specificity, it would be difficult for a spendthrift child to gain access to his share of the estate for squandering.

Minors & Disabled: "Tenth"

Every state requires that a parent (or parents) support, educate, and provide health care for children until they become of legal age in that state. In addition, some states require continuous support and medical care of disabled children even after legal age. In many cases, a disabled child can deplete the family resources, leaving little or nothing to bequeath to other children. Thus, each testator has to decide on some point at which he has fulfilled his legal and moral obligations to his children.

Having minor and/or disabled children imposes the necessity for appointing one or more guardians and conservators. A *guardian* is responsible for the **physical** well-being of a child until the child reaches legal age. After this age, a *custodian* can be appointed to oversee the **financial** well-being of a child until the child reaches the specified age of a testator's choosing. The same person or persons can be appointed as both guardian and conservator.

After the naming and appointment of a guardian and/or a conservator are addressed in the will, it is desirable that the appointments be confirmed by the court. For this confirmation, petitions must be filed requesting *Letters of Guardianship* and/or *Letters of Custodianship*. Having these "Letters" can protect the appointee(s) from false accusations by watchful onlookers, whether family related or not. For example, without the Letters, the taking of a minor child across state lines for vacation purposes could be viewed as kidnapping. Or, the disciplining of a minor child could be viewed as child abuse. The petitioning for Letters provides the opportunity for opposing views to be heard, before the Letters are granted.

With the above comments in mind, let us suppose that a surviving parent has four minor children who are to share in the distributable estate, as follows:

RICHARD (oldest) 15%; ANN (next oldest) 20%;
PHILLIP (disabled) 40%; ESTHER (youngest) 25%
[Total 100%]

The surviving parent is naturally concerned with both the physical and financial well-being of his/her minor or disabled children. After the initial bequeathal wording in the will: *I hereby give, devise, and bequeath* . . . etc., the appropriate paragraph wording might be—

TENTH

Should any of my children be minors at the time of my demise, I hereby nominate and appoint my sister and her husband, namely, ELIZABETH JANE HOPE and WILLIAM THOMAS HOPE, of Baltimore, Maryland, as the Primary Guardians of my minor children, to house and care for them as if they were their own. In the event that ELIZABETH and WILLIAM should be unable or unwilling to act or continue as guardians, I hereby nominate and appoint my brother and his wife, namely, ALLAN KENNETH PHILLIPS and CORINNE LOUISE PHILLIPS, of Houston, Texas, as Ancillary Guardians of my minor children, to likewise act. As each child becomes of legal age, that child's share of my estate (after adjustment for proportionalized consumption while a minor) shall be set aside into a separate custodial account expressly for that child. The custodian thereof shall be any one of the above-name adults preferred by the legal-aged child. The custodian of each said child's account shall seek **Letters of Conservatorship** *under the court of jurisdiction in effect at the time each child attains legal age. With the likely exception of PHILLIP, my disabled son, each child shall be distributed his or her remaining share of my estate upon attaining age 35.*

Bequests to Others: "Eleventh"

Providing for one's immediate family — spouse, children, grandchildren, close kin, etc. — is certainly a testator's primary task. But since it is his property being distributed post-mortem, he can bequeath to other persons of choice. Such persons can be one or more distant relatives, a brother-(or sister-)in-law, a buddy who is a hunting partner, a church "brother" who has been spiritually helpful, a neighbor's teenager showing academic or athletic promise, or just a dear and trusted long-time friend. One or two charities could be added to round out one's sense of moral satisfaction.

Bequests to these persons should be limited to specific property items (relatively low in value compared to property items bequeathed to family members) and to specific dollar amounts (also relatively low in value). For example, said property bequests might be a set of used golf clubs, a damaged sports vehicle, a nonfamous artist's painting, and so on. The pecuniary (dollar) bequests could be $1,000, $3,000, $5,000, or $10,000. Care must be taken to assure that the cumulative value of these "other person" bequests does not exceed about 10% to 15% of the decedent's total distributable estate (after debts, taxes, and expenses). Otherwise, some family member may charge that certain of these other persons exercised undue influence on the testator.

Persons who are not family members are more prone to refuse (decline) items which are bequeathed to them. Such persons may have no need for them, and do not want to get involved in the swapping of items or in their sale. To address this potential, it is a good idea to identify two — what are called *remainder* — persons. A remainder person is someone or some charitable entity who is willing to take anything and everything that no one else wants, when closing an estate. It is preferable that the testator name such persons, but, if not, the executor has discretionary authority to act on his own.

With the above comments in mind, an other persons paragraph might read—

ELEVENTH

I hereby give, devise, and bequeath . . . to the following persons that property and money expressly indicated:

	(Name)	*(Relation)*	*Bequest*	*(Reason)*
1.	_____			
2.	_____			
3.	_____			
•	- - - - -			
•	- - - - -			
X	_____			

Should any of the above persons predecease me, OR should any of them not be located within six months of my demise, OR should any of them refuse to accept the property bequeathed to them, OR should any of them specify acceptance of property other than that bequeathed herein, their bequests shall be null and void, whereupon said property, together with all the rest, residue, and remainder of my estate left unclaimed by any other beneficiary, shall be distributed equally between the following two persons or to the survivor thereof, namely:

CLYDE G. WILLIS and BETTY R. ANTON

The $1 Clause: "Twelfth"

No testator should sign off on a will until he/she has included therein a *$1 clause*. Said clause is also called a "disinheritance" clause, or in more mundane language, a catch-all or shut-out clause. Its purpose is to sweep aside all other claims and allegations that might arise concerning your property dispositional intentions. Only your Last Will and Testament expresses your intentions despite what some out-of-the-woodwork person might say.

Except for one's surviving spouse and minor children, if any, a testator can disinherit any and all of his natural heirs. It is not necessary that there be any particular reason for doing so. A testator is free — after taxes, debts, and expenses — to dispose of as much or as little of his estate to his heirs as he sees fit. He is under no obligation to dispose of it equally, nor is he required to dispose of it according to some percentage formula.

Typical reasons for excluding an heir could be that the particularly-named heir has—

(a)   no financial need for any assets of the testator;
(b)   overborrowed from the testator while living;
(c)   taken on a lifestyle highly distasteful to the testator;
(d)   been mean and obnoxious to the testator; or
(e)   caused the testator undue grief . . . and so on.

Persons other than natural heirs may also be named in disinheritance considerations. This is a prudent course where a known nonheir, such as an ex-spouse, could logically be expected to make a post-mortem claim.

One's disinheritance intentions should be expressly stated in declaratory form. The reason for this is that, after burial of the testator, it is customary to read the will to all heirs named therein. The $1 clause should leave no doubt in their minds as to what the decedent intended.

Let us assume, for example, that John Quincy Jones (previously named) wants to exclude his son, Joseph Scott Jones, because Joseph has a good job and does not need the additional assets. John also wants to specifically exclude his ex-spouse, Margaret Ann

(Moorehead) Jones . . . for obvious reasons. His declaratory $1
clause might read—

TWELFTH

*I have intentionally and with full knowledge omitted to
provide herein for my son JOSEPH SCOTT JONES, as he has
no financial need for any part of my estate. Also, I have
intentionally made no provision for my former wife,
MARGARET ANN (MOOREHEAD) JONES. If JOSEPH or
MARGARET, **or any person or persons other than those
provided for herein**, should prove a right to participate in the
distribution of my estate, to each such person or persons
proving a right to so participate I give, devise, and bequeath the
sum of One Dollar ($1.00) only.*

If one has named and provided for his direct-line heirs and kin
properly, and has provided for one or more close friends, the $1
clause could read—

TWELFTH

*I have intentionally made no provision for any person other
than those named in this Will, whether such person claims to be
an heir or kin of mine or not. If any person or persons other
than those provided for herein should prove a right to
participate in the distribution of my estate, to each such person
or persons proving a right to so participate, I give, devise, and
bequeath the sum of One Dollar ($1.00) only.*

How much more clear can a testator be? The $1 clause
provision has been court tested many times. It is rock solid. With
respect to the recipients of property, such a clause leaves no doubt as
to what the testator intended.

The Witness Paragraph

In order to validate a will after the death of its testator, the
document must be witnessed. We'll explain why in a moment. In
the meantime, we want to point out that the witnessing paragraph is

NOT NUMBERED. There are two reasons for this. One, like the preamble paragraph, the witness paragraph is set by custom. Its wording is stereotyped.

The second reason is that there is no distribution of property expressed in the witness paragraph. It is merely the witnessing of the testator's own signature, and the witnessing of his/her state of mind at the date of signing. It is self-evident, or should be, that a witness must not be someone who is a recipient in any way to any of the testator's property. A witness must be a witness to the testator's signature only. A witness must not be allowed to read the will . . . only its very last paragraph: IN WITNESS WHEREOF.

The stereotyped wording of the witness paragraph reads as follows—

IN WITNESS WHEREOF, I have hereto set my hand this 31st day of January, 2005.

(signature of testator)
JOHN QUINCY JONES

The foregoing document consisting of 5 pages, including this page, was on the date hereof by JOHN QUINCY JONES, the maker thereof, signed in our presence and in the presence of each of us, and at the time of subscribing said document he declared that it was his Last Will and Testament, and at his request and in his presence and in the presence of each other, we have subscribed our names as witnesses thereto.

(Signature of witness)   *Residing at*_____

_____

(Signature of witness)   *Residing at*_____

_____

Note that we show spaces for two witnesses to observe and sign. The two must not be husband and wife. They can be neighbors and friends, but not close family members of the testator. Only one live witness is needed to prove the will. Two are prudent in the event that one is out of town when proof is needed, or should one witness predecease the testator.

A will should always be prepared as an original and one copy. In other words, *two* wills. Both the original and the copy should be signed in the original handwriting of the testator and his witnesses. This way, the second will becomes a "conformed copy." It can be legally substituted for the original upon competent testimony that the original was lost or destroyed.

Your will is of no benefit to anyone else while you are alive. No one is going to steal it. You cannot be sued for statements in it. Keep the original in your own possession, readily accessible. Put it with your "important papers," but **not** in a safe deposit box. Filing it there makes access to it impossible during nonbusiness hours. A will should always be available for reviewing it from time to time.

Give the signed *copy* (the second original) to your executor or other person not living in the same building as you. If you place it with your executor, there is no need to seal it. In fact, it may be advisable for your executor to read it ahead of time. If you give it to someone other than your executor, do seal it. Then clearly label the package or envelope so it will not be forgotten.

ABOUT
THE AUTHOR

Holmes F. Crouch

Born on a small farm in southern Maryland, Holmes was graduated from the U.S. Coast Guard Academy with a Bachelor's Degree in Marine Engineering. While serving on active duty, he wrote many technical articles on maritime matters. After attaining the rank of Lieutenant Commander, he resigned to pursue a career as a nuclear engineer.

Continuing his education, he earned a Master's Degree in Nuclear Engineering from the University of California. He also authored two books on nuclear propulsion. As a result of the tax write-offs associated with writing these books, the IRS audited his returns. The IRS's handling of the audit procedure so annoyed Holmes that he undertook to become as knowledgeable as possible regarding tax procedures. He became a licensed private Tax Practitioner by passing an examination administered by the IRS. Having attained this credential, he started his own tax preparation and counseling business in 1972.

In the early years of his tax practice, he was a regular talk-show guest on San Francisco's KGO Radio responding to hundreds of phone-in tax questions from listeners. He was a much sought-after guest speaker at many business seminars and taxpayer meetings. He also provided counseling on special tax problems, such as divorce matters, property exchanges, timber harvesting, mining ventures, animal breeding, independent contractors, selling businesses, and offices-at-home. Over the past 25 years, he has prepared well over 10,000 tax returns for individuals, estates, trusts, and small businesses (in partnership and corporate form).

During the tax season of January through April, he prepares returns in a unique manner. During a single meeting, he completes the return . . . *on the spot!* The client leaves with his return signed, sealed, and in a stamped envelope. His unique approach to preparing returns and his personal interest in his clients' tax affairs have honed his professional proficiency. His expertise extends through itemized deductions, computer-matching of income sources, capital gains and losses, business expenses and cost of goods, residential rental expenses, limited and general partnership activities, closely-held corporations, to family farms and ranches.

He remembers spending 12 straight hours completing a doctor's complex return. The next year, the doctor, having moved away, utilized a large accounting firm to prepare his return. Their accountant was so impressed by the manner in which the prior return was prepared that he recommended the doctor travel the 500 miles each year to have Holmes continue doing it.

He recalls preparing a return for an unemployed welder, for which he charged no fee. Two years later the welder came back and had his return prepared. He paid the regular fee . . . and then added a $300 tip.

During the off season, he represents clients at IRS audits and appeals. In one case a shoe salesman's audit was scheduled to last three hours. However, after examining Holmes' documentation it was concluded in 15 minutes with "no change" to his return. In another instance he went to an audit of a custom jeweler that the IRS dragged out for more than six hours. But, supported by Holmes' documentation, the client's return was accepted by the IRS with "no change."

Then there was the audit of a language translator that lasted two full days. The auditor scrutinized more than $1.25 million in gross receipts, all direct costs, and operating expenses. Even though all expensed items were documented and verified, the auditor decided that more than $23,000 of expenses ought to be listed as capital items for depreciation instead. If this had been enforced it would have resulted in a significant additional amount of tax. Holmes strongly disagreed and after many hours of explanation got the amount reduced by more than 60% on behalf of his client.

He has dealt extensively with gift, death and trust tax returns. These preparations have involved him in the tax aspects of wills, estate planning, trustee duties, probate, marital and charitable bequests, gift and death exemptions, and property titling.

Although not an attorney, he prepares Petitions to the U.S. Tax Court for clients. He details the IRS errors and taxpayer facts by citing pertinent sections of tax law and regulations. In a recent case involving an attorney's ex-spouse, the IRS asserted a tax deficiency of $155,000. On behalf of his client, he petitioned the Tax Court and within six months the IRS conceded the case.

Over the years, Holmes has observed that the IRS is not the industrious, impartial, and competent federal agency that its official public imaging would have us believe.

He found that, at times, under the slightest pretext, the IRS has interpreted against a taxpayer in order to assess maximum penalties, and may even delay pending matters so as to increase interest due on additional taxes. He has confronted the IRS in his own behalf on five separate occasions, going before the U.S. Claims Court, U.S. District Court, and U.S. Tax Court. These were court actions that tested specific sections of the Internal Revenue Code which he found ambiguous, inequitable, and abusively interpreted by the IRS.

Disturbed by the conduct of the IRS and by the general lack of tax knowledge by most individuals, he began an innovative series of taxpayer-oriented Federal tax guides. To fulfill this need, he undertook the writing of a series of guidebooks that provide in-depth knowledge on one tax subject at a time. He focuses on subjects that plague taxpayers all throughout the year. Hence, his formulation of the "Allyear" Tax Guide series.

The author is indebted to his wife, Irma Jean, and daughter, Barbara MacRae, for the word processing and computer graphics that turn his experiences into the reality of these publications. Holmes welcomes comments, questions, and suggestions from his readers. He can be contacted in California at (408) 867-2628, or by writing to the publisher's address.

ALLYEAR Tax Guides
by Holmes F. Crouch

Series 100 - INDIVIDUALS AND FAMILIES

BEING SELF-EMPLOYED .... T/G 101
DEDUCTING JOB EXPENSES .... T/G 102
FAMILY TAX STRATEGIES .... T/G 103
RESOLVING DIVORCE ISSUES .... T/G 104
CITIZENS WORKING ABROAD .... T/G 105

Series 200 - INVESTORS AND BUSINESSES

INVESTOR GAINS & LOSSES .... T/G 201
PROFITS, TAXES, & LLCs....................................... T/G 202
STARTING YOUR BUSINESS .... T/G 203
MAKING PARTNERSHIPS WORK .... T/G 204
SMALL C & S CORPORATIONS............................... T/G 205

Series 300 - RETIREES AND ESTATES

DECISIONS WHEN RETIRING .... T/G 301
LIVING WILLS & TRUSTS.. T/G 302
SIMPLIFYING YOUR ESTATE .... T/G 303
YOUR EXECUTOR DUTIES .... T/G 304
YOUR TRUSTEE DUTIES .... T/G 305

Series 400 - OWNERS AND SELLERS

RENTAL REAL ESTATE .... T/G 401
TAX-DEFERRED EXCHANGES   .... T/G 402
FAMILY TRUSTS & TRUSTORS .... T/G 403
SELLING YOUR HOME(S) .... T/G 404
SELLING YOUR BUSINESS .... T/G 405

Series 500 - AUDITS AND APPEALS

KEEPING GOOD RECORDS .... T/G 501
WINNING YOUR AUDIT.. T/G 502
DISAGREEING WITH THE IRS .... T/G 503
CONTESTING IRS PENALTIES .... T/G 504
GOING INTO TAX COURT .... T/G 505

For information about the above titles, contact
Holmes F. Crouch

Allyear Tax Guides

Phone: (408) 867-2628   Fax: (408) 867-6466